IN THE BEGINNING,

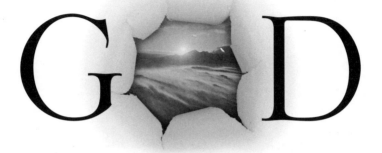

G D

Creation, Culture,

and the Spiritual Life

MARVA J. DAWN

IVP Books
Think Deep. Live Smart.

IInterVarsity Press
P.O. Box 1400, Downers Grove, IL 60515-1426
World Wide Web: www.ivpress.com
E-mail: email@ivpress.com

InterVarsity Press® is the book-publishing division of InterVarsity Christian Fellowship/USA®, a
movement of students and faculty active on campus at hundreds of universities, colleges and schools
of nursing in the United States of America, and a member movement of the International Fellowship
of Evangelical Students. For information about local and regional activities, write Public Relations
Dept., InterVarsity Christian Fellowship/USA, 6400 Schroeder Rd., P.O. Box 7895, Madison, WI
53707-7895, or visit the IVCF website at <www.intervarsity.org>.

Design: Cindy Kiple

Images: torn paper: Terry Wilson/iStockphoto
        blowing snow icescape: Doug Allan/Getty Images

ISBN 978-0-8308-3707-6

Printed in the United States of America ∞

Library of Congress Cataloging-in-Publication Data

Dawn, Marva J.
  In the beginning, GOD: creation, culture, and the spiritual life /
  Marva J. Dawn.
     p. cm.
  Includes bibliographical references (p.
  ISBN 978-0-8308-3707-6 (pbk.: alk. paper)
  1. Bible. O.T. Genesis III—Criticism, interpretaton, etc. 2. God
  (Christianity)—Biblical teaching. 3. God—Worship and love. I.
  Title.
  BS1235.52.D39 2009
  222'1107—dc22

                                                          2009011746

P 22 21 20 19 18 17 16 15 14 13 12 11 10 9 8 7 6 5 4 3 2 1

Y 28 27 26 25 24 23 22 21 20 19 18 17 16 15 14 13 12 11 10 09

To Myron,

who brings the truth,

beauty, and goodness

of God's creation

to our home

CONTENTS

IN THE BEGINNING, GOD

The Bible is all about God. That might seem an overly obvious point with which to begin a book on character formation, but, if we consider the matter seriously, we discover that we often read the Bible imagining it is about ourselves.

One way to ponder this is to contemplate the underlying question we usually bring to the Bible. Often we ask ourselves as we read, "How does this apply to me?" or "How will I live out this text?" Less nobly, we might be subconsciously asking, "How can this text make me feel good?" or "How can I use this passage to support my own ideas?" (since we sometimes read other books or journals that way). Notice that the focus has shifted away from God to us.

What would happen if instead we first asked such questions as these: "What is God doing in this text?" or "What is God revealing about one or all of the Triune Persons in this passage?" It might seem like a small matter, but it is actually an enormous shift in perspective. It is the move from self-improvement to adoration.

OUR NARCISSISTIC CULTURE

As we shall explore in chapter sixteen, the very essence of sin is narcissism, but that tendency to be "inward-turned" or "curved in on oneself" (as Martin Luther described it) is especially aggravated by

our present culture. We are pounded all day long with advertisements (unless we take great care to avoid them) urging us to acquire
what we each "must have" to make our selves happy, or more beautiful, or more in touch with the virtual world, or more in control of our
lives (and often the lives of others).

Each of these goals, in turn, inflames the narcissism further. For
example, to concentrate on making our self happy undoubtedly is to
enter a never-ending quest, since such a focus takes us away from the
involvement with God and others that brings true Joy. Even if Christians don't try to gain happiness by acquiring advertised goods, we
might fall to our culture's dominant ethos by efforts to be comfortable (even in worship!), to be healthy (an ensnaring quest for those
with chronic illness or handicaps, or those with a "need" to be super-
jocks), to be secure (especially in these perilous times), or to be suc-
cessful (an unreachable goal because no marks of measurement are
ultimately gratifying).

The other goals previously suggested similarly lead perpetually to
dissatisfaction and thereby drive us to continued pursuit. An overem-
phasis on outward beauty is often accompanied by a failure to develop the sort of inner character that can discover contentment, so
we constantly need new cosmetics or clothes to make us remain extra
fashionable. All the gadgets of our increasingly virtual world lead us
to ever greater superficiality in relationships and, consequently, to
perpetual efforts to find intimacy. To be in control of our lives is im-
possible because of the many factors—economic, physical, social,
and so forth—that affect us from outside our ability to manage them;
as a result, we find ourselves having to multiply our efforts to regain
mastery of our life. We could go on at length to consider the various
temptations to narcissism piqued and aggravated further by our culture, but let these few comments suffice to awaken us to the realization of how easily our daily lives are pushed toward self-centeredness
and how readily, subsequently, we bring that focus on ourselves to
our Bible reading.

KEEPING GOD IN THE BEGINNING

You might agree with me that Christians too easily tend to be self-centered even in our study of the Scriptures and that our present culture inflames that tendency, but you might still wonder about my remark at the beginning of this chapter that to ask how a Bible reading applies to us is to misread the Bible. Isn't that the way serious Scripture students have always been taught to approach a text? Haven't we all learned these three basic questions for analyzing the Bible: "What does the passage say? What does it mean? How does it apply?" What could be wrong with approaching the texts that way?

In chapter three we will consider an alternative method for immersing ourselves in biblical texts, but at this point let me simply say that the problem with the three-question approach is that it doesn't always start in the right place. We can too naturally tend toward asking what the text says and means for our benefit instead of what it says about God, and how its purpose ultimately is to draw us into worship.

An example of starting in the wrong place comes from *The Prince of Egypt*, the wonderfully animated movie of the Exodus. A song in the film says, "Miracles can happen if you believe." Such a reading of the story leads us to renewed efforts to believe harder so that we can experience miracles.

The Bible, however, paints an entirely different picture. Exodus points out specifically that Israel complained and doubted and cried to the LORD in terror up until the time that they received the gift of the LORD's deliverance.[1] Not until after the Israelites saw God's great work in which the Egyptians were dramatically destroyed does the text say that "the people feared the LORD and believed in the LORD and in his servant Moses" (Exodus 14:31).

The text's structure urges us to focus on God. Once the pitiful circumstances of the Israelites have been sketched (Exodus 1–2), the whole narrative of the Exodus is full of verbs that show God in action. The people's horrible situation in Egypt began to be changed because of this: "God *heard* their groaning, and God *remembered* his

covenant with Abraham, Isaac, and Jacob. God *looked* upon the Israelites, and God *took notice* of them" (Exodus 2:24-25, emphasis
added). Before we start asking how such an account might pertain to
our own lives, then, let's be sure to examine deeply what God does
and what the text reveals about God's character.

THE LEPERS AND THE WIDOW

I am sorry that I can't find the source of the following illustration so
that you could read its particulars, but several years ago I saw a summary of the results of a research project comparing Bible studies in
two different kinds of churches according to their wealth. The project
findings demonstrate how important it is for us to keep God in the
beginning of our reading.

The researchers discovered, as the members of rich and poor
churches studied Jesus' healing of lepers, that more wealthy group
participants talked about how they could contribute to the healing of
the "lepers" in their neighborhood and larger community. In star-
tling—and more truthful—contrast, Christians from poorer parishes
knew that they were the lepers in need of Christ's healing.

Wealthy Christians concentrated first on how the text applied to
them and spurred their actions, but they failed initially to focus on
what God does to heal us all. If we know fundamentally how great
God's healing is and, derivatively, how much we all need the Trinity's
actions in our lives, then we will certainly be more compassionately
able to minister to others and to pass on God's healing.

One more example can perhaps make very clear the necessity of
keeping God at the beginning of our Bible study. Almost every time I
have heard a discussion of Jesus' parable of the "persistent" or "impor-
tunate" widow (Luke 18:1-8), the result has been some sort of moral-
ism. If we focus on the woman and think of her as badgering the judge
unceasingly until he finally gives in and responds to her plea, then we
will learn from the parable that we should keep pestering God until
He[2] changes His mind. But that is to misread Luke's introduction to
the parable and the specific way the story is structured.

If Jesus told His disciples this parable "about their need to pray always and not to lose heart" (18:1), He wouldn't describe a God who is like the judge in the story that follows. Why would we want to pray to a God like that?

Rather, the text reiterates three times that this was an unjust judge "who neither feared God nor had respect for people" (v. 2; see also 4, 6). Because of his injustice, the poor widow was constrained to hassle him. This judge is meant to be seen as a blatant contrast to our merciful and gracious God, who indeed cares about us, even before we ask!

If we begin our study of the parable by looking for what it tells us about God, we will notice this sharp turn: the Lord says, "Listen to what the unjust judge says. And will not God grant justice to his chosen ones . . . ? Will he delay long in hearing them? I tell you, he will quickly grant justice to them" (vv. 7-8a). That is why we do not give up on prayer—not because we are capable of pestering God until we get our way, but because God is faithful to listen and bring about justice.

The parable's chief point is that God is gracious and ready to hear our cries. We do not have to change God's mind; He is absolutely *not* like that judge, and He hears us immediately when we call to Him. Jesus encourages us to be persistent in prayer, not so that we can persuade God to our purposes, but so that God can accomplish His purposes in us. The issue for us, when we finally get to the end of the parable, is whether or not we have trusted the God whose character the story emphasizes by telling of His opposite. Jesus asks this final question: "When the Son of Man comes, will he find faith on earth?" (v. 8). Grateful faith will be there if we keep looking to God's steadfast persistence rather than to our own always-inadequate attempts in prayer.

HERE, IN THE BEGINNING, GOD

In this book we will be paying particular attention to what Genesis 1–3 tells us about God so that we will respond with adoration. You might want to set this book aside for a few minutes to scan those three chapters and pay attention to all the verbs that have God as their subject. What a great gift it is to us to notice just in the first creation account all the ways that God created, said, saw, separated, called, made, set, blessed, finished, rested, hallowed! How can we not but praise our magnificent Creator for all His works?

POSTMODERN PHYSICS AND THE "LAW" OF WORSHIP

A few years ago a friend of mine who teaches at a community college in Washington State gave me a hilarious report of a lively interchange following a guest lecture delivered at the school. According to her account, a postmodern speaker was lauding the death of Newtonian physics. He claimed that this earlier science, based on the laws of universal gravitation and motion formulated by Sir Isaac Newton (1642-1727), had been entirely oppressive, only the work of dead white males. Of course, it is true that quantum mechanics and other twentieth- and twenty-first-century developments radically changed our views of much of physics, especially concerning the importance of relationships more than the specifics of individual quarks or neutrinos.

However, no matter what questions the audience raised, the speaker kept insisting that *all* of Newton should be replaced. Finally, one brilliant woman (who even understands Stephen Hawking!) decided to take a comic approach. She said, "Yes, you're right. We should celebrate the death of everything we've ever learned from Newton. We could cancel all classes and have a party." The speaker eagerly agreed. "Then," she continued, "you could cap the event and demonstrate that Newtonian laws no longer apply by jumping *up* from a thirty-story building."

No matter what revolutionary insights we have gained from the new physics, the law of gravity still generally holds true on many levels. I confess to not knowing enough science to be able to say how much it applies, but, as we all ordinarily observe, apples fall down from the tree, airplanes land, gravitational pulls hold planetary orbits reasonably steady, and, to our great grief, World Trade Center towers collapse.

I use this universal *Law* to illustrate the grounds for my comments in this chapter related to this book's purposes. There is a Law in the cosmos from the beginning of God's creation that relates to human culture, and that is the Law of Worship. The germinating idea for this perspective came from a 1997 lecture by Harold Best, at that time dean of the Conservatory of Music at Wheaton College. Let me quote him at length to establish the vision out of which my comments on Genesis 1–3 will come:

> There is no one in this world who is *not*, at this moment, at worship in one way or another, consciously or unconsciously, formally or informally, passively or passionately. This is a law of worship fully at work which cannot be understood without a double inquiry into how God originally created us [and the world] and how the darksome mystery of the Fall cut into the beauty of His work. For there is a [Newtonian[1]] law of worship, a common ground law of worship, authored by the Creator Himself from the eternities. This law was then turned upside down and into a lie by Satan, but thanks to the indomitable force of Truth and the finished work of Christ, this law can once again be turned right side up. This law can issue in two kinds of worship: that of death unto eternal death or life unto everlasting life. For the question is not, When do we worship . . . ? Instead, it is, Whom do we worship and with what condition of heart?[2]

The goal of the Christian life is that for more and more seconds of each day what we think and do and say is to God's glory, that every moment is worship of the true God instead of various idolatries of our making or of our culture's. With regard to that culture, which for our purposes here will be defined as all the products and results of human creativity, the question is whether our creations of culture are invented, constructed, and used in genuine worship of God.

As we look closely at Genesis 1–3, let us keep constantly in mind that the issue is worship. Many people who read this passage fail to keep this issue central and therefore ask the wrong questions, for the biblical accounts of the Creation and the Fall are not meant to be a science textbook. They are not intended to ask the *What?* and *How?* of biology or astronomy or the *When?* of prehistory.

No, these chapters are meant to ask the *Why?*—and the answer is, for the glory of God. That is why the Fall in Genesis 3 is so deadly, for human worship due to God becomes corrupted, and worship by the whole cosmos becomes distorted. But I jump ahead of myself.

The very structure of Genesis 1 underscores its adoration—and the first worshipful dimension of the structure that strikes us is how much the text is focused on God. The name *Elohim* is actually the plural form of the name *el* or "god," to suggest that Israel considers its God the "God above all gods." *Elohim* (or simply "God" in English) occurs thirty-five times in Genesis 1:1–2:3, and we should note momentarily that this number is a multiple of seven. Its particular significance for us at this point lies in reinforcing our awareness that the poet of this text gives continually recurring praise to God for all the splendors of creation.

The dazzling wonder of that praise was brought richly to my ears one evening at a hymn festival. A masterful poet read the text of Genesis 1:1–2:3, and the timbres of her voice and the thoughtfulness of her cadences sparked in us a new listening and a refreshing openness. Meanwhile, an ingeniously nimble organist played the text—with twinkling flute stops for the stars, whirligig trills and swoops of string sounds for the seeds and plants, rushing cascades of oboe and clarinet pipes for the insects and birds, ranks of blatant brass for the beasts, and a stunningly contrasting silence for the Sabbath, with a royal stateliness for the conclusion. His bustling inventiveness exhilarated us and transported us with wonder to an invigorating new earth. For many of us there that evening the occasion was perhaps the site of our deepest worship ever with this text.

Intentionally, then, the Bible begins with an arresting focus on God—teaching us not only that this is the way we should always read the sacred text (as we learned in the previous chapter), but also that the purpose of Genesis 1 is to call us into similar worship. I doubly accentuate this because our tendency to read in the wrong direction often leads us to problematic attitudes about texts. Instead of our responding to them with adoration, our presuppositions can generate such unhelpful comments as "This doesn't fit with what we know about science" or "I don't understand this!"

God wouldn't be GOD if we could always understand Him. The One whose ways are not our ways does not have to make sense to us. It is a habit of modernity and modernity's sureness that science can explain everything that drives us to expect immediate comprehension of all matters. The escalation of technologies in our society has trained us to assume that all confusions or problems can be fixed. We start with ourselves and human accomplishments, and we want God to match up to our image of Him. When a biblical passage shows us new dimensions of God, we think the text is wrong, rather than we ourselves.

If while reading we ask what a text teaches us about the Trinity and God's workings, then we will begin with a proper humility and end with the praise that God deserves. We will grow increasingly to acclaim God for what we do understand in texts, for we are astonished at what He has done, and we are freshly grateful. Regarding whatever we can't comprehend, we will be content to wait with confidence for growth in insight and faith by God's gracious gifting. Starting with God enables us not to have to try harder or to question God, but frees us instead to abide in trust, to rest worshipfully.

That is not an irrational stance—to set aside judgment because a person realizes that "God is GOD, and we are wee," as I like to say. Two valuable gifts of postmodernity are its questioning of how we know what we "know" and its greater openness to mystery. Both these attitudes can lead to worship of an inexplicable God. Rather than idolizing our own intelligence, we will with reverence yearn for the Trinity's revealing of truth.

But then what can one believe? About what can a person be sure? Genesis 1 wants to tell us, "Look around and see." When you see the wonders of the earth and sky, don't you respond with greater gratitude to their Creator, increased praise to God? The first chapter of the Bible wants to woo us into honoring the Mighty One who brought all of creation into existence—namely, "God"—and it suggests that the rest of the Book will tell us enough about that God to warrant constant trust and confidence, according to the Law of Worship in which everything was made.

3

GENESIS 1:1–2:3 AS LITURGY

Congregations are in the habit of distinguishing themselves from those in other denominations or groups by calling their styles of worship "liturgical" or "nonliturgical." In truth, however, there is no such thing as a nonliturgical worship service, unless all of the time is spent watching professional performances. The Greek word *leitourgia* is comprised of the words for the "people" (we derive the word *laity*) and [their] "work." To be liturgical is simply to include ways for the attendees to be involved. The liturgy might be as plain as "songs, sermon, songs" or as elaborate as a full mass, with all the elements of the ancient rites, but usually those who are present participate in various ways in the work of worship.

Liturgy is an ordering, so that the people know how to participate. Sometimes a liturgical cue can be an embellished change of key and guitar introduction that tells people which song is coming next; maybe it is a quotation from Scripture to which the people respond with the other half of the verse. Perhaps participants have learned in the past how to chant a psalm responsively or to bow reverently toward the altar before and after entering the area that surrounds it. Many worshipers have been "traditioned" after a Scripture lesson to answer the proclamation "The Word of the Lord" with the shout "Thanks be to God!"

Part of the liturgy in many African American churches includes any of a number of affirmations that the congregation members call out after rousing sentences—phrases like "preach it!" or "hallelujah!" or "you go, girl!" (One of the exclamations you don't want to hear is "bring it on home," suggesting "enough already.") Another piece of liturgy could be the repetition of a key phrase in the preacher's sermon (much like the refrains politicians set up in their convention speeches).

REPETITION OF KEY PHRASES

The latter is the kind of liturgical refrain that might have attended the reading of Genesis 1, if not auditorily at least in people's heads. As we listen, we notice a repeated pattern for the days. Aside from the particular details of each day's productivity, the narrator repeats these four phrases in almost every day's description: "And God said," "And it was so," "And God saw that it was good," and "And there was evening and there was morning, the first [or whichever] day."

We catch their rhythm and begin to chime in on the refrains in our minds. Last summer when I was teaching about this liturgical rhythm in Genesis 1 at a Bible camp, participants in my sessions made up a skit about my class for the "talent" show. They wrote and performed a rap song with one of the refrains being "God said, it came to be, it was good, evening and morning." (Another refrain in their rap, which will appear again in chapter four and others, was "recapitulation of the cosmos.")

When there is a definite pattern in a work of art (whether that be a painting, a poem, or a piece of music) and suddenly something changes, it startles us, and we try to discover why the artist intended it. Often we never find out, but the shift wakes us up from our mental slumbering or sloth. If we are careful persons, we will want to imagine some of the possibilities.

For example, in the second day of creation, we don't encounter the phrase "And God saw that it was good." Can this mean that the firmament wasn't good? But wait—there is an unusual phrase, "God called the dome Sky." What is so important about that dome that it is given a name as important as the "Day" and the "Night"?

Sky is like a roof over our heads. It is like a womb in which the earth safely dwells. As the world's ozone layer has started to deteriorate, we now know that it provides a protection from harmful rays. Of course the Sky is good.

Thinking about it has increased our gratitude. We know how important the Sky would be to the biblical desert people and is now to us. Especially if we have heard this text before and know that the refrain is *always* repeated for the other days, we want to inform the narrator/storyteller, "Wait! You've forgotten something." In our minds we add the necessary phrase, "And God saw that it was good." This liturgy has caught us up into participating.

GOD SAID; IT CAME TO BE; IT WAS GOOD; EVENING AND MORNING

If you repeat that rap refrain (the title of this section) several times, giving one beat to each of the four phrases, it starts to grow in you. It fulfills the two criteria that we have discussed in the first two chapters of this book, for it helps us focus on God and what God did, and it moves us to worship.

What an extraordinary God we have! He only needs to speak, and something comes into existence. As Psalm 33:9 tells us, "For he spoke, and it came to be; / he commanded, and it stood firm." Furthermore, what comes to be is good. Finally, there is a security in the ordering of evening and morning. There is a stability in the fact that evening and morning have from the beginning of time continued to follow each other in perfect succession. Certainly a God who creates such goodness and the assurance of an enduring sequence must be caring, as well as powerful.

This fundamental dialectical truth that God is both good and almighty has issued in the basic argument people have against God when they suffer from illness or troubles. They question if God could be both good and almighty if evil can still happen in the world. If the afflictions come, God must not be mighty enough to prevent them, or else God is strong enough but not good enough to stop them. Since that assumption is so pervasive in our culture, it is significant that the Bible commences with praise for these truths about God. If we begin with trust that God is indeed both good and almighty, then we look elsewhere for the reasons behind suffering. (That is not our main purpose in this chapter, but we will consider the matter again later in chapter seventeen.)

THE ORDERING CONTINUES

Just think how crazy life would be if you went to an apple tree and found oranges on it or if ladybugs reproduced as flies! Aren't we grateful that the Genesis 1 liturgy contains the line "Then God said, 'Let the earth put forth vegetation; plants yielding seed, and fruit trees of every kind on earth that bear fruit with the seed in it'" (v. 11). Unless human beings deliberately cross-pollinate or the winds or bees cause a mix-up, we can usually count on apple trees yielding apples and ladybugs generating more ladybugs to land on our fingers and give us moments of delight.

My point is not to get into complex horticultural issues, but to increase our praise to God that, in general, life follows the ordering God commanded at the beginning of the world. God said that it was good, and the general ordering of creation continues to be good for us, because we can usually depend on the customary patterns of the little things in everyday life.

We customarily don't notice the ordering unless something upsets it—the seas transcend their borders, the heavens withhold their water. Then we complain and ask God why. But perhaps this chapter can help to restore our praise for the original good design of everything God made.

EMPHASIS ON LITURGY

At this point, let us return to the comments in the previous chapter that the Bible was never meant to answer the *What? How?* and *When?*

questions of the sciences and prehistory, but to lead us to the *Why?*
that is answered, "For the glory of God!" Actually, the questions cannot be too neatly divided, for they all depend on the largest mystery
of *Who?*

Furthermore, simply to split the questions into those for biology,
astronomy, physics, and so forth, leaving faith with the *Why?* seems
to me to give too much to science. It is to say that the statistics of a
biological analysis of a certain species is more important that the fact
that each unique bird is created for God's glory. Science, for example,
does not know all the *How?*s of the bird's singing. It might know the
mechanics that make its song possible, but it has not yet figured out
all the recipients and solicitors of its communications.

I love the sciences—I had a great time learning about the many
kinds of ladybugs and apples before writing the section above—but
they always lead me to worship because it seems unbelievable to me
that all the unfathomable intricacies of fruit and the fruit's defending
insects could have happened randomly. The question of *Who?* does
encompass all the other questions, even the whole world of science,
because all the discoveries of that world lead us to worship.

Perhaps my all-time favorite of God's creatures is the hummingbird. I bought myself a present of a calendar of hummingbirds so I
can enjoy looking at them every day of the year. They are utterly astonishing. Some kinds are less than three inches long; some are four.
They weigh only a few grams, even less than a penny, though the
smallest kind, the bee hummingbird, weighs only 1.95 grams, or 0.07
ounces. Yet they flutter their wings up to 78 times a second to hover
over a flower, and their wee hearts beat more than 200 pulses a min-
ute. How can such minuscule creatures fly nonstop across the Gulf of
Mexico (at least 800 kilometers or 500 miles)? But the ruby-throated
hummingbirds do so annually.

All the scientific facts, though incredible, are nothing compared
with the indisputable enchantment of watching one or more. Last
year a pair of hummingbirds nested in a tree in our front lawn, and
they tolerated our presence as we observed them and their fledglings.

One iridescent male even seemed to be saying goodbye on the last day we saw any of them, as he hovered, looking into our faces near the large back window.

WHAT IS THE POINT OF SUCH BEAUTY?

What is the point of all the beauty in the world—dramatic views from mountaintops or toward them, copiously colored sunsets over heaving oceans or placid lakes, millions of pastel wildflowers dancing in the wind? Why spend time pondering the intricate brightness of the tiny hummingbirds?

The point of beauty is to display the glorious creativity of God. The point of pondering it is to heighten our worship.

The purpose of noting it in this chapter on liturgy is to prevent silly fights or scientific doubts over Genesis 1–2. Science does not disprove praise, nor does the Bible's beginning claim to be an explanation—rather than exultation. The opening liturgy draws us into wonder and adoration because in the darkness of void and emptiness the Trinity continues to be present and to speak to create, to cause brilliant beings to appear.

SCRIPTURAL FORMATION

You are what you eat," the saying goes, and to some extent it is true. If we eat nutritionally, we are more likely to be in better health. However, sad to say, some people in our society don't think much further than food when they consider what or who they are becoming. They think they are free to design their own future, but don't realize the many cultural pressures that propel them into various conformities.

Instead, let's remember the saying of Thomas Merton: "Your life is shaped by the end you live for. You are made in the image of what you desire."[1] Having learned in the previous chapters to begin our readings with God for the goal of worship and having seen how the liturgy of the Bible's beginning draws us into deeper praise, now we are ready to think about how worship and Scripture reading form us in the image of the God for whom we yearn.

It is part of the Law of Worship, discussed in chapter two, that every human being longs in one's deepest self (often hidden by stacks of ambitions or piles of debris from a rough life) to be in relationship with God. Merton gives the example "To be an acorn is to have a taste for being an oak tree."[2] That is a very recognizable symbol here at our home, for when the squirrels plant in our yard acorns from the mammoth oak tree in the yard behind, my husband is soon digging up little oak trees to put in pots to give to friends. We check two seedlings' progress in the yard next door; now they're about fifteen feet tall.

Created in the image of God, we human beings want to be like God. (The trouble arises when we want to *be* God, but we'll discuss that later.) Since in Jesus "all the fullness of God was pleased to dwell" (Colossians 1:19), we look to Him to know the way to live. We long to have His character and all the virtues inherent in it.

As background, then, to other chapters in this book, it is necessary to make this chapter foundational like the first three. How are we formed to have the character of Christ and, through Him, that of the Triune God?

Primarily, we acknowledge that we can't do it; we can't make ourselves into someone who thinks, speaks, and acts like Jesus. By grace, the Holy Spirit works to form us through the positive influences that surround us—chiefly the gifts of creation, the Word of God, and other members of the Christian community.

When we perceive the ubiquity of beauty in the world, we ache to be an agent of beauty in the lives of those we encounter. When we abide in the Word of God, we are sculpted by it increasingly to correspond to its narratives and descriptions of virtues. When we have a community to point out our weaknesses and to hold us accountable for our habits, the Spirit uses their proddings and prunings to stimulate new growth.

But we need a community of people who all fervently desire to follow Jesus. Together we can support each other in resisting the powerful forces of the culture that would pull us into its violence, greed, consumerism, addictions, mindlessness, and passivity.

THE CHRISTIAN COMMUNITY IS AN ALTERNATIVE SOCIETY

We will see more clearly as this book develops why it is essential that the Christian community be such an alternative to the society around us, but here we should simply note that to follow Jesus will put us at odds with the culture in many dimensions of our lives. Here we want to focus on this alternative being offered by a genuine community.

I was overjoyed when the NRSV finally translated this verse more in keeping with its Greek original: "If anyone is in Christ, *there is* a new creation" (2 Corinthians 5:17, emphasis added). It is not simply that "he is a new creation" or "she is a new creature," but that everything is different, and all of us together make that new creation visible, to display for the rest of the world what is possible when we live in union with Christ.

It is not that we are better than everyone else, that we are more holy or clever. It is that we know the power of forgiveness and live by the Spirit's work within us to participate in what God is doing in the world. We know where we are headed—toward the "recapitulation" of the cosmos, "putting the Head (Jesus) back on" the restored creation, the culmination of God's eternal reign at the end of time—so we hold on to a confident hope in the Trinity's future. Meanwhile, we have the privilege (and the calling, which engenders responsibility) to be God's ambassadors, proclaiming the Good News of God's cosmic lordship and serving as agents of God's purposes in the world.

This emphasis on the alternativity of the Christian community does not endorse a "we-they" mentality. We stay vigilant against becoming moralistic or fantasizing that we are superior to others.

Rather, to accentuate that the Christian community is an alternative society calls us to humility, for indeed we cannot live well on our own. We desperately need Christ's deliverance and the Holy Spirit's empowerment to live truthfully, in accordance with the Father's creation.

As an alternative society, we Christians in the community nurture each other, and especially our children, differently. Each of us and all of us in the community care about helping each other and our youth to hold biblical values. We want others constantly to know that God's instructions give us the best choices for the way to live. We invite everyone to delight in nonconformity, to rejoice in the Spirit's transforming work in our lives. We begin to train our children with worship and hearing the Scriptures when they are very little, for we long for them from the earliest time possible to discover the goodness of God's design, the truth of God's instructions, and the Joy of following them—not as duty, but as glad response to God's profoundly loving revelation and invitation, the Trinity's mercy and grace.

FORMATION OF CHARACTER

How is character formed? All parents want to know the answer to that question, for certainly they wish their children to turn out well. And, indeed, we each want to know, for we all have aspects of ourselves that we would like to change, character traits that bother us. Every one of us is a sinner, so without doubt we could all use a bit of an overhaul in our personal makeup.

But character formation does not have invariable procedures of cause and effect. Too many factors surround us in our milieu to guarantee any specific results. But throughout the Bible we find guidance for what we want to become. We've already seen from Genesis 1 that we read the Bible from the perspective of looking to learn what a text tells us about God and what God does, that the goal of all our Bible reading is worship, and that texts are meant to invite our participation in them. To what else should we pay attention for the sake of our character formation and the formation of others'?

1. More than rules or goals. Many people think of the Bible as a set of rules by which a person should live. Though the Scriptures do contain many of God's statutes, especially the Ten Commandments, these are not meant to challenge us to keep "trying harder" to comply with them. In fact, sometimes rules do just the opposite. For example, some children rebel against their parents' rules simply to provoke them.

The biblical commandments begin with a statement of grace, that the LORD giving these instructions is the one who first brought His people out of slavery in Egypt, that His merciful deliverance now frees them to respond to mandates with obedience. The focus, then, is not so much on the rules themselves, but on the kind of people we want to be. Moreover, the motivation lies not in the rules as laws for behavior, but in the positive invitation of God's grace and in the delightful results of obedience.

Nor does the Bible contain a specific goal or end toward which we should strive—for example, as some people think, that the Scriptures tell us how to get to heaven. God's Word offers more than a simple reward that we aim to reach; instead, it speaks of eternal Joys that are given to us as God's gifts. Again, the root of everything is grace. We would all die in despair if our lives depended on our ability to reach the goal, because we all know that our sinfulness prevents our perfection, and to please God requires nothing less. Instead, God is pleased out of His character of mercy, rather than because of our flawed character.

2. Grace leads to desire, and desire leads to character. The more richly we know God's grace (and I mean "know" in its Hebrew sense that includes intimacy), the more our desire for God grows. And as we learned from Merton at the beginning of this chapter, we are shaped by what we desire.

This is true also for grace as it comes to us through other people. As they exhibit certain noble virtues that we might be lacking, their very possession of those attributes increases our desire for them. This is especially true in my marriage. I want very much to grow to become the kind of considerate and thoughtful person that my husband, Myron, is. It is in his nature, his character, to be observant of others' needs and to work immediately to meet them. He is the first to acknowledge that these character traits come from God and not from himself.

Notice again that God is at the root of everything, for all the virtues that we admire are *in* God in the first place, and God is the Maker who puts the desire for them in us. We are created to care about what kind of people we are becoming. The rules and goals of the Christian community are part of the narratives that help us to ask questions about character, and, as we read the whole Bible, it shows us many examples of both bad and good characters to increase our desire for the latter.

3. *Behaviors build character.* Let us recognize that life is a spiral. Certain behaviors will arise out of a certain kind of character, and that behavior reinforces the character. If I want to be a kind person, I need Christ to live in me by the Spirit's power to choose kind acts that will develop habits that lead to a character that possesses such virtues.

We can think about the character-building nature of our behavior triunely. For example, suppose an individual had the bad habit of using a nasty word every time something went wrong for her, but then she became a Christian. Each time that, by the Spirit's power, she chooses to say a meaningless word or, even better, remains silent, she works against the old habit and builds on the new. She is aided by remembering that Christ lives in her, and she is sure that He would never say the nasty word that formerly characterized her. Similarly, she does not want to offend her Father and Christ. The more she keeps the Trinity in mind, the stronger she grows in choosing different behavior that is building her character to be more gracious in her speech.

4. *What disrupts nurturing character?* Especially because we live in a milieu that bombards us unceasingly with false notions about ourselves, our money, our time, and our behaviors, we want to be very intentional to foster biblical perspectives in ourselves and others.

We must ask precise questions about our milieu. Its comprehensiveness can be illustrated by comparing a fish, which must live in a milieu of water in order for its gills to draw out oxygen, with human beings, who must not be submerged in water in order to breathe. We thrive in various milieus according to the kinds of people we are—I thrive in a conference setting, while Myron flourishes in a garden.

Moreover, all the factors of our environment affect our development. If a fish swims in toxic water, it will die. If we eat a poisoned fish, we will become ill. Youth in our society are growing up in a poisoned milieu of violence, sexual exploitation, consumerism, and technological bombardment. How can young persons and adults choose peacemaking, chastity, simplicity, justice, and community when we are exposed constantly to unbiblical values in conversations, music, print, and high-tech media.

Those of us who care will take seriously the requirement to create an alternative milieu. We dare not let the moral indifference of our society immobilize us. In turn, the world around us desperately needs what the Christian community has to teach about godly character.

5. *The Christian community as a nurturer of character.* Have you ever noticed when visiting convalescent centers regularly that you can tell which residents are married to each other—not only because of their affection, which has grown golden over many years, but also because, after living together for a long time, they have all of each other's mannerisms and idioms.

With the apostle Paul we can observe the same phenomena in our communal relationship with Christ: "But we all, with unveiled face, beholding as in a mirror the glory of the Lord, are being transformed into the same image from glory to glory, just as from the Lord, the Spirit" (2 Corinthians 3:18 NASB). Notice that this happens more richly because "we all" behold Jesus together and become like Him as the Holy Spirit transforms us into His likeness.

The Christian parish nurtures that transformation by various means. In the congregation's worship and Bible classes we discover and contemplate the narratives that teach us who the Trinity is and what God's people are like in response. In the community's fellowship we encounter the embodiment of those virtues. In the church's discipline we are admonished and cautioned and educated and loved when we choose values other than those of God. In the congregation's strength our courage is fortified to continue embracing the truths that we know about God in the face of postmodern negations of truth and of biblical narratives. The more facets of the Christian community's life contribute together to nurture the development of godly character the more thoroughly the congregation provides an alternative milieu. But this certainly can't happen automatically; such provision must be intentional and consistent and pervasive and strong and beautiful to provide an appealing alternative to our society's milieu.

6. *The narratives that form us.* Throughout the rest of this book we will be asking careful questions about the attributes of character we want to nurture in others and in which we ourselves long to grow. How does God's Word guide us to see these virtues? What qualities are displayed? What has been revealed by the biblical accounts about God's people in their relationships with each other and with God? What mandates are issued that we ignore to our peril? What idolatries are particularly dangerous?

Though we are especially attentive only to Genesis 1–3 in this book, Jesus makes clear in the New Testament that God is triune. Because the Scriptures are inspired by the Holy Spirit to be unified, we believe that Genesis 1 hints at the Trinity, long before anyone knew any specifics.

Genesis 1:2b has been translated "and the Spirit of God was hovering over the waters" (NIV); Eugene Peterson renders it, "God's Spirit brooded like a bird above the watery abyss" (*The Message*). Also, the Gospel of John calls Jesus the Word (1:1-18), and the writer of Colossians joins John in reporting that all things were created through Him (Colossians 1:16; John 1:3), so the Maker's speaking brings us Christ before the incarnation. Most suggestive of all, Genesis 1:26a reveals God saying, "Let us make humankind in our image, according to our likeness." (We will look at some implications of this declaration in chapter six.)

This book is not the place for a full discussion of the Trinity, but it is important to introduce the topic here, since the narratives that form us are those of the Triune God. We grow into the kind of character that God intended for us because Christ dwells in us by the Spirit's power to the glory of the Father. We behold the Triune God in the biblical accounts, and we want to become like Him.

7. *All to the glory of God and the good of the world.* You might not agree with everything in this book. That doesn't bother me, unless you disagree with the book's major purposes. This book is just a beginning to try to get Christians not to fight about Genesis. I pray that

you will go beyond it to ask new questions about the texts and their implications, to develop a Christian community that nurtures godly character in all of us, to offer hope to those drowning in our society's toxic milieu. Most of all, may everything bring glory to the Trinity and draw us into unceasing worship.

5

The First Six Days

As we learned in chapter three of this book, the first major section of Genesis (1:1–2:3) is structured liturgically, so let us begin this chapter with worship. This is the prayer provided for use after Psalm 148 (which you might want to read aloud before speaking this prayer), a psalm which echoes the first creation account in its summons to praise:

> God Most High, by your Word you created a wondrous universe, and through your Spirit you breathed into it the breath of life. Accept creation's hymn of praise from our lips, and let the praise that is sung in heaven resound in the heart of every creature on earth, to the glory of the Father, and the Son, and the Holy Spirit, now and forever.[1]

If the fire and hail, snow and frost, and stormy wind extol the LORD by fulfilling God's commands, let us adore God with our whole beings for all the wonders He has made.

In his lovely book *In the Beginning There Was No Sky*, Walter Wangerin Jr. comforts children by telling them that God loved them so much that after He made light, He created a sky to protect them from the emptiness of the universe.[2] Let us thank God with all that we are for the phenomena that make our environment a livable place to be and fill our lives with enjoyment and elation.

THE ACCOUNTS OF CREATION

If the Bible had been divided into chapters in the sixteenth century, rather than by Archbishop Steven Langton around 1227, Martin Luther would have made sure that the first division was set after Genesis 1:2. He separated the first general description as a first creation account different from the second stages wherein God spoke.

Though I don't know who first recognized it or when, now in the twenty-first century scholars generally agree that the section Genesis 1:1–2:3 should be kept together as a unity because then all its positive nouns are in multiples of seven (see chapter ten). Genesis 2:4 begins a second account that specializes in the creation of men and women with their unique relationship.

THE LITURGICAL FIRST ACCOUNT

As we have discovered, Genesis 1:1–2:3 is liturgical, a hymn of praise—so let us ponder this first section in that way. I will name and muse about aspects of the creation in the order in which they appear, conclude each description with the phrase "O come, let us worship," and encourage you to respond (either vocally or silently but with a moving mouth), "We praise you, Creator, for all that is good."

Let us practice: God created the heavens and the earth. In the entire cosmos of the Trinity, God has created for us a special habitation.

O come, let us worship. ["We praise You, Creator, for all that is good."]

GENESIS 1:3-5: THE FIRST DAY

Were the days twenty-four hours long, and were there exactly six of them? Or did the original Hebrew word *yom* signify aeons (as it does in other places in the Bible) and a sequence? What is essential is that the answers to those questions don't matter for salvation, so we shouldn't exclude anyone from our fellowship who doesn't believe as we do. Truly, I believe that God is so powerful and good that the Trinity could have created the entire cosmos in a day or two.

What actually matters is that we accentuate the praise and thanks.

The Trinity is the source of light, without which we couldn't see to enjoy all the astonishing marvels of God's work, without which we could do nothing ourselves. God also separated the light from the dark and gave us the rhythm that He called Day and Night.

Let us praise God that our earth has never lost its rhythm of days and nights, evenings and mornings. Let us shout for gladness that God, our Light, and God's created light are always good.

O come, let us worship. ["We praise You, Creator, for all that is good."]

THE SECOND DAY: VERSES 6-8

We live on an earth originally created to safeguard us by its firmament. What a wonder it is that precisely on this planet we have the right amount of oxygen to breathe, moisture for rain and snow, atmosphere that burns up falling asteroids, an ozone layer for protection. How glad we are that God created Sky!

What grace it is that the atmosphere hasn't fallen into the sea, nor has the ocean rebelled against gravity and climbed into the heavens. God's separation of waters from waters has continued from the beginning and made our earth an inhabitable home.

O come, let us worship. ["We praise You, Creator, for all that is good."]

THE THIRD DAY: VERSES 9-13

What a gift that God separated the waters from the land and appointed the Earth on which we live! How can we ever thank God for the divine gathering of waters into the diversity of all the raindrops in the world, all the snowflakes and hailstones, the fogs and the mists, all the creeks and ponds and puddles, all the glaciers and snowpacks, the streams and rivers and fjords, the wells and underground springs, the lakes and the bays and the mammoth oceans. How amazing it is that water in general keeps its boundaries so that vegetation can flourish.

And such a variety of vegetation! My husband has scores of kinds of flowers in the gardens around our home. Oodles of them constitute diverse categories of blooms that flourish simply to delight the eyes. At no time in the whole year is there not at least one kind of flower blossoming. Some flowers develop into fruit—apples, cherries, strawberries, raspberries, loganberries; others into multiple kinds of vegetables or seeds that produce grasses or shrubs or trees.

How much the Trinity is to be honored for the waters and land and vegetation! Let us thank God that plants bear seeds and fruits according to their kinds, that we can expect bananas from banana trees and cantaloupes from their seeds in the ground.

O come, let us worship. ["We praise You, Creator, for all that is good."]

THE FOURTH DAY: VERSES 14-19
How could we survive if the Earth did not continue to rotate around its sun? Wouldn't it be a mammoth loss if we did not perceive the beauties of our moon's monthly patterns and a marvelous universe full of stars? How stagnant the world would be if the moon didn't influence the tides! How much life would be lost if the fluctuating tides and inflowing rivers didn't oxygenate those waters to keep sea creatures and sea plants in harmony.

How good it is that the sun is for a sign of God's grace, for seasons and days and years. What a treasure that we arise each morning to a new day, a fresh start. What a delight that most of our living places have four seasons to bring a variety of vegetation and colors and crops, that the fresh and beautiful life of spring always follows the cold and hibernations of winter.

O come, let us worship. ["We praise You, Creator, for all that is good."]

THE FIFTH DAY: VERSES 20-23
How intriguing our world is with its hosts of swarming creatures, its flocks of birds with myriads of shapes and songs, its sea monsters that plough the deeps. How harmonious it is that fish continue to swim upstream to spawn and birds fly south for the winter, that peli-

cans don't reproduce dolphins and whales don't try to ascend into the air beyond their breaching.

How gracious it is that birds and butterflies multiply to fill the Earth with every hue and tint imaginable. How amazing the fruitfulness of spawning fish! How sweet and faithful the trilling of the birds! How astonishing the diversity of bugs and beetles—all necessary for their particular functions in the harmony of creation!

O come, let us worship. ["We praise You, Creator, for all that is good."]

THE SIXTH DAY: VERSES 24-25

How multitudinous are the varieties of beasts and creepers and cattle, how diverse in their sounds, how exhilarating in their appearance, how remarkable in all their gifts to us. What a magnificent design it is that domestic and wild creatures continue to multiply, especially the microscopic organisms that inhabit our bodies to our benefit—and that they multiply according to their kinds. What a rude awakening it would be if the bacteria that aid our digestive systems would reproduce as mosquitoes.

How graceful the running of gazelles! How majestic the roars of lions! How preposterous the shapes of hippopotami, of giraffes, of anteaters!

And yet this is only a part of the sixth day. But the rest is a phenomenon to itself, as we can tell because God ends the creation of the beasts with the liturgical phrase "it was good." (Because the creation of male and female is set off in the text, we will save discussion of it for the next chapter.) Since the untamed and tamed beasts are so astonishing and precious to us, let us glorify God with resounding acclaim for all the gifts of land creatures.

O come, let us worship. ["We praise You, Creator, for all that is good."]

Say it again for the gifts of the week. O come, let us worship. ["We praise You, Creator, for all that is good."]

THE CREATION OF
HUMAN BEINGS

The creation of human beings is also set apart from the rest of the first six days in that God begins by speaking to God's (triune) self. What the Godhead says in this internal conversation is so important that we should look closely at every section of this verse:

> Let us make humankind in our image, according to our likeness; and let them have dominion over the fish of the sea, and over the birds of the air, and over the cattle, and over all the wild animals of the earth, and over every creeping thing that creeps upon the earth. (Genesis 1:26)

That sentence has enormous implications for us all. It gives rise to many questions that affect our theological understandings. In this chapter we will consider the first part of verse 26 and its fulfillment in verse 27, while the last two-thirds of verse 26 will be explored in chapter seven.

THE IMPORTANCE OF *ADAM*
First, before we discuss our main subject, we should note two things about the use of the word *humankind*. One is that the Hebrew word

behind this translation is *adam,* which is the generic word for "earth creature," since *adamah* means "ground." We won't get specific terms for a man and a woman until Genesis 2.

The second point is how essential it is that we translate *adam* generally here. Otherwise, we miss that, in completion of this internal conversation by God, the Trinity makes *adam* as both male and female in the next verse.

GOD'S IMAGE AND LIKENESS

We already noted briefly in the previous chapter that the Trinity is suggested by this verse, though not delineated. What does God mean by saying, "Let us" and "in our image and according to our likeness"?

Those plural phrases made little sense to me until about a dozen years ago when I heard Greek Orthodox Bishop Kallistos Ware propose, "Prayer is eavesdropping on the Trinity." Scholars often say that the Orthodox East and the Catholic West need each other to understand the Trinity, because the Greek language enables the East to envision better God's Oneness (His "substance" in English), while the Latin *persona* has caused the West to concentrate more thoroughly on the Three (separate) Persons.

When Susan, one of my best friends, was serving as an emergency doctor in Rwanda not too long after the genocide there, I was too overwhelmed by her danger to be able to pray for her—until I thought about Bishop Ware's recommendation. Imagine the Father talking about how much He cared for all His children killed in the violence and how grateful He was that the doctors and nurses serving there were bringing the likeness of His care to all the victims of both the Hutu and Tutsi sides of the massacres.

Similarly, envision Jesus saying that He loved all the people so much that He had died and risen to make forgiveness possible in this horrible situation. He especially indwelt the Christian doctors and nurses who were engaged there and was working through them to bring His healing not only to people's bodies, but also to their minds and hearts and souls. And, again, conceive of the Holy Spirit commenting on the empowerment being made available to the medical people so that they could work seemingly unbearable long hours with such gentleness and patience.

The particulars of that conversation are not as significant as the realization of how thoroughly my friend was embraced in her perilous situation by the unfathomed love of the Three in One. Furthermore, to imagine listening to the Trinity helped me to recognize that God is such a mystery that we will always have more to learn, that we can never comprehend but can ever believe that God is One God, but Three Persons.

The experience of envisioning made clearer to me also what it means to be created "according to [their] likeness," for I knew Susan's heart, her will, and understood how she devoted her life to serving refugees in war-torn Africa. Listening to her talk about her work and observing her intensity and passion had in the past made me catch a wee glimpse of the incomprehensible dimensions and mysterious ardor of God's love for the cosmos. In that Susan is like God, her life always points to Him and His ever greater attributes and actions to deliver and restore His children.

Bishop Ware's practice of prayer benefits us especially in asking what it means to be made in God's image. Genesis 1:27 records poetically,

> So God created humankind in his image,
>   in the image of God he created them;
>   male and female he created them.

No matter what other suggestions scholars make about the meaning of being "in the image," they all agree that it includes being in relationship. Since the image is plural and includes male and female, human beings emulate the Trinity in conversation and in working together with common goals. This section of Genesis deals only with what I call "social sexuality";[1] "genital sexuality" is not introduced until Genesis 2 (see chapter thirteen).

Let us pause a moment to acknowledge that Genesis 1:27 provides a crucial answer to those who think that the Bible is patriarchal. The culture that surrounded the writing and compilation of the Scriptures certainly was quite male dominated, but numerous places in the Bible counter that tendency and make the Scriptures very much an alternative. It is especially significant that here God's image is bequeathed equally on male and female, because this text (and other passages that we shall note in the future) was written without any qualifications and was placed at the very beginning of the canon when God's people, by the guidance of the Holy Spirit, formulated the order and contents of the biblical books. God and God's people intended explicitly to name both male and female as equal bearers of God's image.

Next, because the emulation by human beings of the Trinity is always only fragmentary, we see the results of the Fall (see chapter sixteen). Though we are created in God's image, that image is damaged, tarnished, diminished, but not eclipsed. Since the image of God was both male and female, we believe that in the Trinity are to be found all the best characteristics of male and female and more. God is beyond gender, although the One Person who became incarnate had to come as a man, in order to overthrow the false stereotype that women only were the ones who served sacrificially. Because we are made in the image of God, then, we find our best selves as male and female in God.

All the people in the 1960s who said, "I've gotta be me!" made a ruinous blunder in turning inward in their search for fulfillment, for, as Augustine said so truly, our spirits will be ceaselessly restless until we find our rest in God, in whose image we are made. Now, some fifty years later, fallen culture acts to take our masculinity and femininity away from imaging God by attempting to force them into the molds formed by advertising and movies.

We are liberated from all stereotypes about our being male or female, for we find our own unique way of being one or the other by the way in which we image God. For example, my husband is an extraordinary nurturer, a characteristic more often associated with women. (I laughed uproariously just now when I looked up the word *nurtur-*

ing in my computer thesaurus and its six entries were "female, feminine, gentle, ladylike, tender, womanly"!) But during his career of teaching elementary school, his attribute of such deep and compassionate care was profoundly effective in the cases of scores of children with troubled home lives. Now he brings his nurturing and artistry to the fruitful gardens in our yard, and he delivered his rich attention and assistance to me last fall when I broke my femur. I see the image of Jesus in him all the time.

A final aspect of being in the image of God pertains to the Law of Worship that we discussed in chapter two. Again, as Augustine's famous prayer reminds us, we will never be satisfied until we are brought into total union with God. That unquenchable thirst for relationship with and in the Trinity, to worship God utterly, seems to me the foremost consequence of being made in His image.

This sense of being made in God's image calls us all constantly to look for it in others and to do what we can to help them acknowledge it and to realize it by joining in worship. We thereby carry to others the answer to their inmost longing, a yearning for union with the Trinity, a thirst to respond with adoration to the God who made them. Thus, our Christian lives are formed with a deep desire to reflect God's image in our lives to God's glory and to pass on the gracious news of our creation in that image for the well-being of the world.

FORMATION FOR
ECOLOGICAL CARE

There was a time in the 1970s, when the ecological crisis in the United States had become very apparent to scientists and non-professionals alike, that many people blamed Christians for understanding erroneously the last part of Genesis 1:26, which reported God saying that human beings were to be given dominion *over* the fish and birds and all other creatures. Then, after humans are created in verse 27, God blesses them and commands them to

> Be fruitful and multiply, and fill the earth and subdue it; and have dominion over the fish of the sea and over the birds of the air and over every living thing that moves upon the earth. . . . See, I have given you every plant yielding seed that is upon the face of all the earth, and every tree with seed in its fruit; you shall have them for food. (vv. 28-30)

Surely, ecologists thought, such texts had caused Christians to exercise inordinate power over the creatures and thus to contribute dreadfully to ecological damage.

I remember this blaming of the Christians very well because I was in seminary at the time and first learning Hebrew. I noticed that the preposition that is rendered "over" in verses 26 and 28 was the Hebrew letter *Beth*, which is usually translated "with." Consequently, I asked my Hebrew professor if the phrases wouldn't be better interpreted as "have dominion *with* the fish" and so forth. He acknowledged that this would be a good possibility. When I asked why, then, the English Bibles continued to retain the use of "over," he said that he didn't know, but guessed that it had always been done that way in English. Though my ability to use Hebrew is extremely inadequate, I'm still campaigning to get the translation changed to "with."

Just imagine what a difference it would make in the earth if we Christians always understood that we are to have dominion *with* the creatures, that together we would continue to live in the harmony that is suggested by the structure and rhythms of the Genesis 1 liturgy. What would happen if we translated "dominion over" with "leadership in harmony with" instead? But the world is fallen, and now in the twenty-first century humankind's destructive dominion *over* the creatures is grotesquely illustrated by the cruel treatment of cattle and pigs, chickens and turkeys in mass-production "factory farms."

A STRONGER ARGUMENT

A better argument against ecological devastation than my questioning of a preposition is the fact that human beings are made in the image and likeness of God. Thus, if in the beginning we were given the fundamental instructions to "subdue [the earth]; and have dominion," we are to fulfill those mandates as God would—totally nondestructively, but with cherishing and reverence and tender consideration.[1] The Trinity would subdue and have dominion for the sake of all the creatures and the earth.

Since the animals and birds were given the same directive to "be fruitful and multiply," it seems important that the additional instructions were delivered to human beings so that they would use their intelligence to manage everything so that the harmony of the creation would be preserved. It appears that Genesis 1:26-29 provides the best ecological education possible: act in the stead of the Creator in such a way that none of the carefully constructed intermingling and cooperation of the cosmos would be undone.

TAKE IT PERSONALLY

We should also notice that the text adds a significant phrase when the assignments are given to human beings. God speaks "to them." In personal relationship with the male and female made in His image, God blessed them (as He had the creatures in verse 22) and then talked with them directly. The Trinity gave humankind the responsibility to care for everything that moved in the waters, through the atmosphere, and on the land, and for the appropriate administration of the food supply (more on that in the next chapter).

These responsibilities are reinforced in the second creation account, the beginning of which is signaled by Genesis 2:4 and by the addition of the name LORD, the covenant name, to the term *God* throughout the rest of the chapter. Though we will not at this point look at the unique creation of man and woman, what we want to focus on here is the *inclusio* of the narrative of the garden—prefaced by "and there was no one to till the ground" (2:5c NRSV) and concluded with "The LORD God took the man and put him in the garden of Eden to till it and keep it" (2:15 NRSV).

How could Christians miss it—as some have in the past and still do! Our first instructions as God's people were to nurture the gardens and animals of the creation. We have been environmental caretakers since the beginning.

AN AGRICULTURAL CONTEXT

As we read the Bible we want to remember the context of the various writings, and in the case of the beginning of the Bible the setting is obviously agricultural. As the account in Genesis 2 makes manifest by the use of a Hebrew construction, the original *adam* is especially tethered to the ground *(adamah)*. I can understand that best by watching my husband.

Over the course of living on this same piece of land for twenty years, he has become intimately tied to the soil. He knows the limits of our property and the possibilities for its flourishing. He recognizes the places that need much more compost; he knows the plots that drain more quickly. He works with the properties of each section—how much sunshine it gets, where it is easier to water, what grew there last year. He doesn't overstrain any part; he lets sections go fallow in turn.

Most people in our society, however, are not so attuned to the ground. They spend their time in offices or on airplanes and do not recognize how much farmers and gardeners cooperate with their animals and/or soil. As a result, many folks do not conceive of the biblical meaning of "dominion." They don't understand the patience the land and creatures require. They don't realize that it takes years to be truly informed about the properties of all kinds of vegetation and animal life. Only genuine cultivators of crops and animals love their creatures and therefore truly care for the well-being of all.

I see that in the times when Myron allows plants to remain in the garden long after they've turned to seed, so that the birds can eat; in the times when he walks outside and stands still—gazing lovingly at the plants; in the times he spends planning what has to be done for each part of the land and why and when. And the lessons that Myron has learned from the land are applied to the people he encounters. He deals with everyone with intense interest, patient gentleness, and attentive care.

My husband has shown me that God's first call to humans to be gardeners is also a spiritual calling. Just as we attempt to be careful in our tilling and keeping of Eden so that in God's likeness we nurture it, so we want to be fulfilling our vocation as God's image in our spiritual and moral formation. Practices of ecological awareness and action will build in us the kind of disciplines that are helpful for our formation in spiritual character as well.

Other biblical passages in which we can immerse ourselves for ecological appreciation and formation include Psalm 148, Job 38–39 and 40:15–41:34, Matthew 6:10b, and Luke 12:27-28. We can also spend time immersed in both the beauties of nature and its present ecological problems—both by viewing areas of disharmony and destruction and by reading the literature about the devastation and what we can do about it.

TWO FINAL NOTES

As we look at the description of the Garden of Eden, or Paradise, we are dismayed to realize that it was located somewhere in or near the area now known as Iraq. Certainly we want to do all we can to restore this ravaged land and its people. War is one of the greatest causes of ecological violation, of massive assaults on the harmony of creatures and soil. In whatever ways we can contribute to peacemaking, we also impart gifts for the safekeeping of the animals and their habitats.

Genesis 2:10-14 is careful to recite the names of the four rivers that flow from the river coming out of Eden. We are immensely grateful that a river of the water of life is part of the scene of God's final paradise, the New Jerusalem (Revelations 22:1-2). When God brings to its culmination the reign of His kingdom, the water and trees will serve for the healing of the nations.

Meanwhile, however, the earth is facing a global water crisis of monstrous proportions. More and more areas of the world are facing severe droughts or massive flooding. New record-setting typhoons and hurricanes add to water's devastations. Witnessing and reading about these shortages and torrents call us to continue our vocation as keepers of the earth by working to provide wells, sanitation projects, supplies of water, and rebuilding assistance for those victimized by these afflictions.

From the New Testament we learn that Christ indwells us and the Holy Spirit empowers us so that we are formed to live to the glory of the Father. To be ecologically minded does not paralyze us with hopelessness. Instead, the Trinity fills us with Joy as we participate in God's work to restore creation's harmony to the earth.

FORMATION FOR JUSTICE

Next month the congregation to which we belong is joining other church communities and groups of justice builders across the nation to write letters to legislators to urge them to pass specific legislation that will work toward an adequate food supply throughout the world. This "Offering of Letters" is one way to get more people involved in actions that lead to genuine justice.

The Offering is sponsored by the bipartisan agency Bread for the World.[1] Being a Christian organization (one I highly recommend you become involved in), Bread uses as the biblical basis for its call for letters the narrative of Jesus multiplying the loaves and fishes to feed the crowds. Just as Jesus offered the little food that He had and thousands were fed, so we turn our faith into actions, and our actions are multiplied because God uses them.

There is great hope for the world as more and more people are formed to be workers for justice. It is exhilarating to know that God's design for global justice is actually written into the first creation account at the beginning of the Bible.

DESIGN FOR JUSTICE—BEHOLD!

The Trinity's intention that there be justice in the world is stated to human beings in this way:

> Then God said, "Behold, I have given you every plant yielding seed that is on the surface of all the earth, and every tree which has fruit-yielding seed; it shall be food for you; and to every beast of the earth and to every bird of the sky and to every thing that moves on the earth which has life, *I have given* every green plant for food"; and it was so. God saw all that He had made, and behold, it was very good. (Genesis 1:29-31a NASB)

(The phrase *I have given* is in italics in the NASB because it is assumed in the original Hebrew text, but not specifically stated.)

I used the NASB in this chapter because it keeps the double use of the word *behold,* an imperative for which the verbs *see* or *look* are inadequate alternatives. Even worse is when English translations ignore the command entirely. "Behold!" is meant to be a grab-you-by-the-shirt-collar shout, so that we readers wake up and pay exceptionally diligent attention.

The first time "Behold!" is employed, God tells the human beings that He is giving them not only plants for food, but the mechanism by which more plants will be formed. Thus, the human beings have the responsibility not only to make sure that the animals and other humans have enough food, but also to manage the seeds that will produce food for the future.

The second time "Behold!" is utilized, our attention is called to the addition to the usual phrase "it was good." We will consider the addition to the phrase more in the next chapter, but meanwhile let us ponder whether "very" is inserted also because of the possibility for justice in the earth.

BEHOLD! FOOD FOR ALL

It is significant that God moves against selfishness right away in this first creation account. Immediately after proclaiming to the human beings that plants and their means for producing more fruitfulness are given to them so that they have food, God goes on to include all the animals, birds, and creepers in this largesse. All creatures are to have enough food.

God created enough green stuff (and I don't mean money!) for all to eat. (I'm sorry that this joke might not work for readers outside the United States, where the money is all green.) What was so good about God's creation, which is hinted at by the orderliness of the first account, is that everything was inaugurated to be in harmony. With the loving dominion of human beings (within the sovereign care of the Godhead), animals and birds and crawlers were to remain in balance with their environment, and there would be sufficient food for all.

Later, when God chose the Hebrew people to be His own in a covenant relationship, part of that covenant involved the keeping of Sabbath, in which all strangers were welcomed to participate, and the keeping of the Jubilee, in which all lands were to be returned to their rightful owners, so that the rich could not get richer, and the poor would not get poorer. So both the creation mandate and the instructions from Sinai were to contribute to a continuing righteous distribution for all to have enough to eat.

In keeping with the spiritual emphasis of this book that calls us to adore God for His divinely good purposes, we pause a moment here to give the Trinity praise for the original fairness of the earth and that equity toward its inhabitants: Gentle and generous God, we celebrate You for Your righteous dealings with all of us on the globe. Your design for the world is for perfect justice to prevail. Live in us, Christ, and by Your Spirit at work through us re-form us as fervent builders of true wealth throughout the world, so that all may have adequate nutrition and flourish in life. We ask this for the sake of Your glory and on behalf of those disregarded in this unrighteous world. Amen.

RIGHTFUL DISTRIBUTION OUT OF BALANCE

Because human beings are fallen (which we'll consider in chapters fourteen through sixteen), God's plan for upright sharing of the earth's resources has been pitilessly skewed. One reason for human (but not eternal) hope is that the Millennium Development

Goals, on which all the nations of the world agreed, lists as its number-one priority "to eradicate extreme poverty and hunger" by the year 2015.

As I write this, at the halfway point of the year 2008, some progress is being made—but not nearly enough. For the first time since 1981, when the following indicator was first measured, the number of people living on less than one dollar a day has declined to less than one billion. This is an achievement to be noted, because the world's population continues to increase, but the absolute number of persons in poverty actually is decreasing.

However, according to Bread for the World's 2008 statistics, more than 850 million people on the globe still do not have enough to eat. In the United States, which is certainly one of the wealthiest nations, one out of ten households faces hunger at the moment or is at risk of hunger. (This statistic was compiled in May 2008 before the severe economic downturn following the U.S. mortgage crisis and bank failures. Undoubtedly, a greater percentage of homes were then confronting the effects of the food and fuel crisis.)

Distribution is the problem. God continues to provide the seed-bearing plants, but the complexity of the connected issues, such as turning corn into biofuels (why can't we use something other than food to make our fuels?), sometimes immobilizes people and prevents us from working against hunger.

That is why it is so important for each and all of us to contact our nations' governments to ask what our countries can do to participate in fulfilling the Millennium Development Goals, in accord with the rest of the world. Besides that, of course, we can contribute to agencies that verifiably make sure that food and the necessities in materials and personnel for agricultural development get sent to needy places on the earth.

Has anyone asked you lately to make a real sacrifice to help feed others as well as we ourselves are fed? I'm asking you that now, for the sake of honoring God's creation mandate to humankind.

HOW OUR LIVES ARE FORMED FOR JUSTICE

God amazes me with all the different means that the Trinity uses to form us in certain ways. What experiences and biblical texts and print or multimedia presentations can make real for us the immense needs for food in the world and the detrimental effects on everyone because over 850 million individuals live on less than one dollar a day and billions do not get enough to eat? Every five seconds a child in the developing world dies from preventable and treatable causes, and for 60 percent of those who die the cause is hunger and malnutrition. The agony for me is the set of words *preventable* and *treatable*. Why can't we who are the rich of the world be roused to do what we can about it?

We could end hunger! It would take another thirteen billion dollars to meet the basic health and nutritional needs of the world's poorest people: that is *less than* Americans and Europeans spend in a year for pet food.

How will God use us to wake up those who have been unaware that by God's grace His original creation purpose that all should be fed could be realized? It will not be our human accomplishment, for in the end only God can bring His kingdom to culmination—meanwhile, only God sends the rain and the sunshine so that plants can grow. Only God has made plants with seeds for continued multiplication; only God has made the earth and water out of which abundance comes. But God will use us to work toward the goal of ending hopelessness and hunger for those in desperate poverty.

My life was changed by participation in an around-the-world choir concert tour when I was twenty. When we were in India, we saw the large shovels with which sanitation workers scooped up the bodies of the dead on the street to cast them into a cart to be taken to the city dump for burning. The throngs of beggars, the destitute ones waiting outside hospitals, the children wounded by their parents so that they would receive more money from their begging, the overwhelming smells of poverty—these and other signs of desperate deprivation haunted my mind when in the New York City airport a month later a few of us noticed in stark contrast an impeccably groomed poodle with an elaborate bejeweled collar. At that sight I vowed to myself that I would never stop working for the hungry.

That intention was reinforced when I was first learning Hebrew in seminary. My favorite text became this portion of Isaiah 58:

> Is not this the fast that I choose:
> > to loosen the fetters of wickedness,
> > > to unfasten the thongs on the bars of the yoke;
> > and to set at liberty the crushed ones,
> > > and all the bars of the yokes to tear apart?
> Is it not to divide with the hungry your bread,
> > to bring the homeless afflicted into your own home;
> whenever you see the naked to cover the person,
> > and never to hide yourself from your own flesh?
> then your light shall break forth as the dawn.
> (Isaiah 58:6-8a, my translation)

Undoing the fasteners on bars of the yokes and pulling them off meant to me that we get to the roots of things, that we search beneath the surface explanations of problems and find out the underlying causes. Dividing our bread with the hungry meant equal sharing. Perhaps we could divide our grocery budget in halves—one half for ourselves and an equal amount for the needy in the world.

To do that will change the way we eat and constantly remind us that this is the kind of fast God wants—unceasing mindfulness and a lifestyle that keeps the needy at the forefront of our family budgets. From what yokes of bondage and oppression we could set other people free!

That is why I took the pen-name Dawn from the fifty-eighth chapter. I want it perpetually to remind me of the Isaianic call to a proper Sabbath fast that releases the afflicted from their burdens, that meets the needs of the hungry and homeless, that never turns away from any human being who requires our aid. I hope that from now on my last name will remind you of this text from Isaiah 58, too, and of its implications for your own life and the lives of your family and friends.

And it all starts with Genesis 1. God designed a harmonious universe, one in which everyone could eat nutritiously and flourish in all other ways. How did the earth get so unbalanced that if you have food, clothes, and a roof over your head you are richer than 75 percent of the world?

GOOD EXCEEDINGLY!

What is the difference between "good" and "very good"? Perhaps it could be something like "the total is better than the sum of its parts."

This is illustrated by one of the early scenes in the movie *Ratatouille*. A rat who has the attributes and passions of a chef finds some cheese (mmm, good) and some strawberries (mmm, good) in the dangerous kitchen of a woman who will try later to blast the rats out of existence. But when he puts the two tastes together, the fireworks truly begin, and he is transported to a new level of life. The two tastes together offer much more than each one does separately.

If this is the meaning of the difference between the "good" in Genesis 1:25 and the "indeed, it was very good" of Genesis 1:31b, then it would be more than simply a matter of God taking steps in the process of creation until the earth is filled to a suitable extent. If that were the case instead, the word *very* would signify only that now that the last part has been added, the series is completed.

Without doubt, however, the structure of the text tells us that creation is *not* finished. Since all the main nouns in this first account occur in multiples of seven and some of them have not occurred yet in such a number, we are clearly shown that the culmination of God's process and design has not been reached with the human beings.

According to this first account, then, human beings are not the capstone in a series of creations. God must have a different purpose for changing the refrain to "indeed, it was very good."

NOT DEGREE, BUT MAGNITUDE

Other passages that use the same word that we translate "very" might give us a better sense of how the middle phrase in verse 31 should be understood. Hebrew lexicons suggest that the term might better be rendered "exceedingly." We can get the same sense by pondering two other texts in English.

The first is Genesis 4:5b, which is now always translated "Cain was very angry," though the old King James Version renders it, "Cain was very wroth." Once I struggled for a long time with the narrative of Cain because it seemed very unfair of God to refuse to accept Cain's sacrifice. It wasn't until several careful readings in a row finally turned the lights on that I could see how Cain had not come with true worship when he brought his sacrifice. This is accentuated by the contrast with Abel, who, "for his part brought of the firstlings of his flock, their fat portions" (v. 4), whereas Cain had simply taken "an offering of the fruit of the ground" (v. 3).

When God "had no regard" for his offering, and Cain became "very angry" (in *The Message,* Eugene Peterson renders the sentence, "Cain lost his temper and went into a sulk"), God tried to reason with him and woo him to worship in verses 6-7. The LORD warned Cain that sin was "lurking at the door" and that he should and could master it. Instead, Cain let his resentment and animosity fester and grow into the action of killing his brother. His initial anger was excessive, and his pride grew it exceedingly—hence, the tragedy.

Let us also look at a positive example of "very" in Psalm 46:1b. Many translations render the second line of the strophe "a very present help in trouble," but the NEB urges us to take a second look with its version, "a timely help in trouble." That variation makes us ask how else God might be "very present," besides in a timely way. Perhaps we might think of the LORD being present in physical proximity or in tangibility or in power.

The word *very* seems in this case and in the Cain case to indicate magnitude or the measure of something's consequence or supremacy. Cain was so excessively angry that his belligerence controlled his whole life—attitudes, character, action. God is so imminently present that we are embraced by His timely, forceful, and passionate help.

INDEED, IT WAS GOOD EXCEEDINGLY

Therefore, let us consider "very" in Genesis 1:31 in the sense of "magnitude." What in the preceding text (vv. 26-31) might give us a hint as to the significance of this latest creation?

One of the many things that stand out for us is the fact that the creation of human beings is the only aspect of the whole week about which there is conversation within the Godhead. All other elements of the creation account begin simply with God commanding and something coming to be. What might be the purpose of this narrative device?

Almost always when the Scriptures repeat something the purpose is so that we will pay extra (very!) close attention. In this case the dialogue within the Godhead is partly expanded in the description of the creation itself (v. 27), and the larger portion is repeated and added to in the account of God's command to humankind (v. 28). Each section deserves the contemplation in which we've already engaged together in the previous chapters.

We don't need to rehash here that earlier work concerning the image of God, the equality of male and female in bearing God's image, and the ecological and justice implications of verses 28-30. However, it is compelling if we call the contents of those chapters to mind because thereby we learn many reasons why these latest additions to the beings of the earth call forth a new refrain. This is especially important in our postmodern culture.

THE UNIQUE VALUE OF HUMAN BEINGS

Most people who don't acknowledge God as the Creator of the world find no special significance in humankind. Especially because human beings have so devastated God's ecological balance, many environmentalists these days want to degrade us to a position no higher than anything else in the world—as if demoting us will give us any incentive to change into avid earth-keepers! Of course, what they want is that human pride will be stifled and wrongful exercising of "dominion" will cease.

However, what we need is not less biblical formation, but more. To be immersed in the biblical assessment that our creation, along with our God-given abilities for ecological care and justice management, made things "good exceedingly" challenges us to fulfill our role as image-of-God bearers and justice builders. We are motivated to care for the earth as the Trinity does. God, who fashioned the world and redeemed it, certainly will ultimately bring it to the culmination of His design for it in the "recapitulation of the cosmos," the "new heavens and new earth" at the end of time. Meanwhile, He sends rain and sunshine for it and oversees the natural processes of renewal. He gifts scientists with intelligence and imagination to develop appropriate methods for truly replenishing the soil and making growing conditions more productive. He fills compassionate people with zeal to ensure that distribution mechanisms become more equitable.

In addition to the call to live in the image and likeness of the Trinity as we fulfill our mandate for nurturing and protecting the environment and all its inhabitants, we human beings have the distinction that God spoke "to [us]" (v. 28a) as He did to no other. The intimate relationship with the Trinity that God offers to us bestows additional inspiration and incentive for us to heed His ordinance.

Moreover, to obey God's injunctions is a delight to us, for by doing so we worship with our entire lives. In the perfection of creation we want to manage and have dominion over all the beings of the earth in God's stead and in God's way.

DELIGHTING IN OUR CALLING TO BE HUMAN
The previous paragraph is written as if there had been no fall, so that we can ponder the "good exceedingly" of the sixth day. If we would immerse ourselves more thoroughly in the present in the flawless-

ness of God's design at Creation and in the purity of God's purposes for the future fulfillment of the Trinity's reign, then we could and would be formed to rejoice in our calling to be human. Ecological care, peacebuilding, and working for justice throughout the earth would not feel like add-on burdens demanding more time from us than our jobs allow. Instead, we would remember that this is part of what we were created for in the beginning, that we were formed to delight in these pursuits.

Robert Farrar Capon's book *The Third Peacock* describes God as having the utmost of a good time during the creation process. He pictures the Trinity partying and One Person saying to another something like, "There, what do you think of that?" as He tossed out a hippopotamus or an albatross or a giraffe. The other Two would shout "Good!" and offer applause.

Just imagine God's ecstasy, then, when the Trinity made us in their image and likeness, gave us the guidelines of our vocation, and exclaimed in unison, "Good exceedingly!" When we envision that elation over our being and our calling, we cannot help but respond, "O come, let us worship. We praise You, Creator, for all that is very good!"

How would it change the world if more of us were formed to embrace our calling as human beings and enjoyed to the hilt our role as keepers of the earth's balances and builders of global justice?

KEEPING THE
SABBATH WHOLLY

In the previous chapter we discovered that human beings were not the capstone of the first creation account, though the addition of them did bring with it the acclamation "very good." Instead, we wait until the seventh day to encounter the pinnacle of God's design, the Sabbath day. The Jews celebrate her preeminence by calling her Queen Sabbath and by welcoming her with songs and solemn rituals, festivities, and special foods.

The power and purpose and poetry of the Sabbath is underscored by the liturgy's structure. Remember that in chapter two, when we had just begun our explorations together, we mentioned momentarily that the name *God* was used in the Genesis 1:1–2:3 liturgy thirty-five times, a multiple of seven, which in Jewish literature always symbolizes perfection. Throughout the account God does the work, so this hymn or liturgy is full of acclamation for all the wonders God has accomplished. God created, God saw, God separated, God called, God made, God placed, God blessed, God completed. The poet exuberantly celebrates all that God has done in this first narrative by naming God a perfection-multiplied number of times.

Shortly thereafter we found a fluke in the patterns, for, in the second day's narration, the motif of "God saw that it was good" was not used. However, in the previous chapter we noticed that the word *good* is employed twice on the sixth day, so that we still wind up with seven uses of it in the entire liturgy.

The second most prominent noun in the original Hebrew of this whole passage (Genesis 1:1–2:3) is the word *'aretz* or "earth," which occurs twenty-one times (again, a multiple of seven that is only sometimes successfully rendered in English translations). This is a text of praise for God's relationship with the earth, a relationship not only of creating, but also of ordering. Perhaps this multiple of seven also implies that the earth is to be given its Sabbaths, too, as is explicitly mandated in Leviticus 25 and commemorated in 2 Chronicles 36:21.

The words *day* and *light* also occur in multiples of seven, appearing fourteen and seven times, respectively, while the nouns *darkness* and *night* each occur only four times, which for the Hebrew writers symbolized a more earthly or mundane matter. Sevens, which the Gospel of John also uses fervently as a sign of perfection, dominate this liturgy to highlight the stunning gift of the Sabbath.

THE SEVENTH DAY

As we learned earlier in this book, in order for the structural pattern of the first creation account to be complete, the first chapter of Genesis should include also the first three verses of chapter two. These verses complete some significant elements in the structure.

We encounter the twenty-first use of the word *earth*, and the thirty-third, thirty-fourth, and thirty-fifth uses of the name *God,* so the structure indicates that with the seventh day we have reached the capstone of God's design. This is underscored by the announcement in the first sentence of verse 2 that God had finished His work. In Hebrew that sentence is seven words long, and the middle word is the number *seven.*

One of God's actions, which highlights this crown of creation, is to hallow the day, to set it apart as consecrated. We will consider that more intensively in the next section.

The announcement of the second half of verse 2 introduces the idea of God resting as a model to be followed. The verb for resting is actually the root out of which the name *shabbat* comes; it emphasizes not only resting, but also stopping or ceasing. The number *seven* comes from a different Hebrew root. But the fact that the two words appear together in the same sentence gives Christians the charge to honor those who observe their Sabbath on the seventh day.

We remember that the early Christians were all Jews who kept the Sabbath on the seventh day and then began also to observe the eighth day, or the Lord's Day, because of the resurrection. Only when Christianity began to be increasingly separated from Judaism was more emphasis put on Sunday as the special day of worship.

THE SANCTIFIED DAY

Genesis 2:3 gives a quite simple description of God's sanctification of a holy day: "So God blessed the seventh day and hallowed it, because on it God rested from all the work that he had done in creation." This text implies that the motivation for keeping a Sabbath is in imitation of God.

Since we are reading Genesis 1–3 to see how God forms us through these chapters, we recognize that the first creation account does not tell us much else about Sabbath keeping than that to practice it is to imitate God. That alone would be sufficient reason, of course, but God has given us also many texts from Exodus, Leviticus, and Deuteronomy to flesh out more of the reasons why Sabbath is such a gift and more of the details concerning genuine Sabbath observance. We also learn various practices from Jewish legends, songs, and traditions.

What we do draw for our formation from this text is that to keep a holy day is written into the very fabric of creation. Since the entire first creation account culminates in the seventh day of God's resting, that model is an essential core of the whole earth's being.

For this reason I believe it is highly significant that Jesus kept the Sabbath day carefully. It is true that the Pharisees were scandalized that He healed on that day, but many contemporary Jewish scholars agree that to do so was a rightful observance of the holy day. If the whole point of the day is to give us rest and reprieve from "all the work [we have] done," then a specific gift of restoration would be an appropriate appreciation of the day's purpose.

The early Church seems to have identified and honored Jesus' observance of keeping the holy day because it named the day Jesus spent in the tomb "The Great Sabbath." The compelling practice of Jesus in celebrating Sabbath must have effectively convinced His disciples, too, for they did not come to the tomb to anoint Him that day, though they dearly loved Him and probably would otherwise have gone (Luke 23:55–24:1). This was a commandment still to be kept, though its abuses were later rejected by the apostle Paul (Colossians 2:16-23).

Since the hallowed day is the pinnacle of God's creation and reinforced throughout the Trinity's work of atonement in Christ, certainly it is a precious treasure for us still in our time.

A GIFT FOR THE TWENTY-FIRST CENTURY

Sabbath keeping changed my life. Since it was not a part of my childhood Christian practice, I began to wonder about it when I was in college. It troubled me that Sabbath observation was one of God's great Ten Commandments and yet most Christians didn't keep a whole day.

When I first learned that the structure of the Genesis 1 liturgy climaxed in God's hallowing of the day, it made no sense to me that we didn't practice a holy day. If the Sabbath was the pinnacle to the creation of the cosmos, why has it not retained that significance?

That led me to much deeper study of its details.[1] The study was accompanied by my initial attempts at practicing the keeping of a holy day. The practice changed my life more than the study of it, so I pray that a result of this chapter will be your own initial or continuing endeavors to be true to your creation harmony of six days of work and one whole day of rest every week.

Rick Barger's *A New and Right Spirit: Creating an Authentic Church in a Consumer Culture* offers an insightful image for how much our culture needs the gift of a day to rest.[2] People in our society seem to be addicted to the busy "rat race" that often puts us in slavery. Barger's image for that bondage is that our lives operate as if we are stuck on a merry-go-round, know that we are, and dislike it intensely, but we don't know how to get off. Instead of simply jumping off, we continue to buy more tickets.

Genesis 2:3 tells us how to get off. God sanctified a day and invited us to emulate Him in jumping off the rat-race merry-go-round and resting one day out of seven. The more we practice removing ourselves from the busyness of life for a separate day of ceasing to work and worry, the more we learn to bring that Sabbath *shalom* into the other days of the week.

The great Jewish theologian Abraham Joshua Heschel taught me that Judaism is different from every other religion in the world because the first thing made holy in it (and Christianity consequently) is not a place, but a time. Since the Sabbath day has been hallowed, by observing it we enter into its holiness.

What a gift that is to ourselves, to our churches, and to the society around us! Our fallenness as individuals, as members together in a community, and as a culture is amplified when we ignore the creation pattern of sevens—that we should work six days and rest one. It has made us harried, conflictual, inharmonious, and violent.

God has given the gift of the Sabbath as the fulfillment of the design of His creation. We ignore it to our peril. We celebrate it as a treasured glimpse of Paradise's perfection.

THE SECOND
CREATION ACCOUNT

The November 11, 2006, issue of *Time*, besides an ironic forty-eight-page special section on "The Best Inventions of 2006," featured a scintillating debate between the atheist biologist Richard Dawkins, who wrote the *New York Times* bestseller *The God Delusion*, and the Christian geneticist Francis Collins. The latter was the director of the National Human Genome Research Institute and the leader of the 2,400 scientists who co-mapped the human genetic blueprint, with its three billion biochemical letters.

I rejoiced in the debate because Dr. Collins, most obviously a rigorous scientist, was able to speak strongly about the compatibility of science and Christian faith. When asked whether belief in the resurrection of Christ and other miracles fatally undermines his scientific method, which depends on natural laws, Dr. Collins answered:

> If you're willing to answer yes to a God outside of nature, then there's nothing inconsistent with God on rare occasions choosing to invade the natural world in a way that appears miraculous. If God made the natural laws, why could he not violate them when it was a particularly significant moment for him to do so? And if you accept the idea that Christ was also

divine, which I do, then his Resurrection is not in itself a great logical leap.[1]

Besides affirming his evangelical faith in the resurrection, Dr. Collins also made it clear in the debate that to believe in God as Creator of the world was more compelling than the suggestion by Dr. Dawkins that out of "zillions" of multiple universes one or more could have by chance developed the right six constants to make our globe inhabitable. Those of us who adore God the Creator believe that the six constants, such as gravitational pull, are so finely tuned that they couldn't have happened by accident or random.

Dr. Collins kept insisting in the debate that faith was not the opposite of reason and that it was perfectly compatible with the development of scientific knowledge. That is why in this book we can study the creation accounts for what they are teaching us for formation; we do not have to use them as a science textbook, since science has not yet been able to tell us anything definitive about creation. No one was there to conduct any experiments; therefore, scientists can only posit theories.

THE SECOND CREATION ACCOUNT

If people say that they doubt God's creation of the world because the two accounts in Scripture contradict each other, surprisingly many Christians don't know how to answer. Some believers have never even carefully read the second chapter of Genesis, except for the specific verses about the creation of a man and a woman (2:7, 21-25). If we ponder the text painstakingly, we can unravel the seeming biblical tangles.

A new creation account is signaled by the general statement of Genesis 2:4a (which somewhat parallels the summary given in 1:1) and by the new use of the phrase LORD God (or YHWH Elohim in Hebrew) in 2:4b. This phrase makes use of the covenant name YHWH, which is rendered "I AM" or "the LORD," with its last three letters being reduced-size capitalizations. In the French the custom is to render this word with "L'Eternel."

The Hebrew people never said this personal name for God, which had been given to Moses at the burning bush, because they did not want to blaspheme the holy name. As a result, no one knows for certain how to pronounce it, though scholars are highly likely to have figured it out accurately. We will honor the Jewish custom (and might want to think of developing such a habit for ourselves so that we always extol the infinite holiness of God) by using the unpronounceable four letters (called "the tetragrammaton") YHWH. That way, we will always pause at the word and praise God's covenant faithfulness.

The name connotes relationship. This is the name given by God to assure the Hebrew people that He was their dependable and devoted Guardian, who would bring them safely out of Egypt and into the Promised Land. This is the Promise Keeper, whose steadfast love and faithfulness would unceasingly be with them. This is the true Lover, who persistently honored His side of the covenant, though Israel kept disobeying and turning away.

The use of the name YHWH at the beginning of this account already signals that its purpose is different from that of the first. The first one, with its multiples of seven, climaxes at the end when those numbers are completed in God's creation of the Sabbath. Its structure is one of order and harmony, a liturgy of praise.

This second narrative, in contrast, has a pinnacle at the beginning and then one to match it at the end. Its focus is different. It builds on the notion of relationship—with God and with another and with the whole earth. And it sometimes moves in unusual directions to support that accentuation.

In this account the vegetation was planted by God after the man was created, because the emphasis here is on the human beings as tillers of the ground (see 2:5c). This is to be a lovely garden as a place for them, for it is watered by the rivers rising from the ground.

THE FOUR RIVERS OF EDEN

Four rivers are named as four branches coming off the river that flows out of Eden, but the paragraph about them (Genesis 2:10-14) has been interpreted in several ways. In general the five verses seem to be intended to cite a specific place in which relationships are formed, but the extent of that space might have to be left as a question.

Some speculate that the area designated as the garden by its rivers encompassed the whole of the inhabited world at the time of the writing of Genesis. If that could be the case, then the first river, the Pishon, could be a larger body of water such as the Persian Gulf or even the Indus or Ganges Rivers, which flow down Pakistan (on the west side of India) and the east side of India, respectively. This would make the area called Havilah (meaning "sand") the whole arid area east of Iraq.

Also, the description of the Pishon includes comments about gold, bdellium (a sweet spice or fragrant gum), and onyx stone being found in Havilah, which is thought to be diverse places in Assyria, Babylon, or Arabia by various scholars. Bdellium also comes from the area of India, so these three treasures are not much help for ascertaining the location of the river Pishon.

The other unknown river, Gihon, has raised similar speculation because of the use of the name *Cush* for the land around which the river flows. Some suggest that it might signify the Nile, and this would add part of Africa to the garden area. Thus the names of the four rivers would be used to suggest the world. Others suggest the likelihood of an Arabic Cush, which leads to the proposal of the next paragraph.

More strongly, scholars suggest that the two curious rivers were smaller rivers in the region in which the Tigris and Euphrates parallel each other. Then the four rivers together would indicate a small location in the land that is now known as Iraq (which has been made anything but a garden in the recent years of violence).

Are the rivers valuable to us in reading the Bible, since we can't say for certain what they represent? Yes, I think so. They seem to depict the extent of the known world into which human beings were set or to delineate a particular area where life first flourished. Thereby, we recognize that God provided adequate water (which now is the cause for fights along these rivers), extra treasures of mineral and aromatic wealth, and a location for relationships to be formed.

FORMATION CONCERNING WATER AND WEALTH

We should not take lightly the emphasis the four rivers display concerning God providing plenty of water for the Garden of Eden. Finding an adequate supply of water for agriculture and for personal needs is the source of great anxiety throughout the world, especially in Australia and parts of Africa, and even in many sections of the United States afflicted with drought. Most scholars recognize that future wars will probably originate in water crises, since the world's supply is shrinking, due to increasing population and factors such as changed weather patterns because of global warming.

This element of God's gifting provision could have been added to both our chapters on ecological care and justice (chapters seven and eight), for both are in steep demand today in relation to water. The text acknowledges that water is an endowment from God's largesse, and therefore we know that we are called to be good stewards of it for the sake of the whole earth.

Compared with the rest of the world, residents of the United States seem to waste much more water, except when they are under drought restrictions. Similarly, the exorbitant use of bottled water in the United States and other countries increases ecological damage and trains us not to care about the entire world's water supply. We need a reminder ourselves and can offer perspective to others as we grow more in our appreciation of the great gift that water is to us.

We can foster that growth by joining in efforts to dig wells in needy parts of the world, to provide sanitized water for areas of crisis, and to foster better water preservation practices, such as choosing yard plants that don't require extra watering. We are called to conscientiousness about the amount of water we ourselves dispense and consume, so that we do not waste it.

We do not need to prolong our discussion about wealth here, since we stressed that in chapter eight, but once again the text shows that natural resources are gifts from God. God caused them to exist in the environs of the garden for the sake of the flourishing of humankind. Thereby we cannot make them our private possession, employ them to oppress others, war over them to deprive others, or govern them to defraud others.

As much as it is in our power, let us apportion God's gifts of water and other resources faithfully. When doing so requires more than our power, let us join in efforts to secure reasonable distribution for the well-being of all. This text in Genesis 2 brings to our awareness the unfathomed dimensions of God's gifting as a first step toward trustworthy stewardship.

FORMATION TOWARD RELATIONSHIPS

What is distinct in this second creation narrative is that the placement of the creation of plants (vv. 8-9) and animals (vv. 19-20) is made subservient to the importance of, and commands given to, human beings. Plants are formed to provide a place in which human beings can be put for the work of tilling and keeping. Plants also furnish a place where obedience can be tested (vv. 9 and 16-17).

Animals and birds are made to provide companionship, but their failure to do so completely sets the stage for the great theme of Genesis 2, the creation of man and woman (a different point from God's image being male and female in Genesis 1). To that sublime subject we will turn in the next chapter of this book.

Here we need to underscore that everything in Genesis 2, no matter the order in which it appears, converges to prepare a place for human beings. Whereas the first creation account culminated in the perfect ordering of the world under the care of humankind as displayed in the flawless purity of God's Sabbath rest, this second narrative focuses more wholly on the human beings and their commands in relation to God and to each other.

Perhaps there are hints of the stability needed for such relationships to develop. If so, those glimmerings form us to construct similar balances for the sake of our affiliations. More important, there are specific commands by which we know how to maintain intimacy with God and one another. Those mandates are as relevant now as when they were first given. In fact, the world around us desperately needs to see what it means that Christians keep them.

CREATION OF
MAN AND WOMAN

You've probably heard the old joke about a little boy who heard his pastor say on Ash Wednesday, "Remember that you are dust, and to dust you shall return." A few days later, after looking under his bed for a lost ball, he went to his mother and said, "Mom, do you remember what the pastor said Wednesday night about being from dust and returning to it? Well, under my bed somebody is either coming or going!"

That method of coming or going sounds dreadfully lonely! In contrast, the creation of man in the Bible appears to be an affectionate act of a tender, covenant *YHWH* God, who must have enjoyed immensely shaping the (then) perfect human being. As the footnotes in the NRSV tell us, the LORD formed the man (Hebrew *ha-adam*) from the dust of the ground (Hebrew *adamah*).

Now, if this was the God in a covenant relationship with a particular people later in history, I don't think such a God would nastily kick the dust around or slam it into a glob. The image is rather one of meticulous, jovial, and gentle molding, such as a potter exhibits in shaping an exquisite vessel. Indeed, the verbs used in the first creation account, *create* or *make,* are not used here. This is a special instance of God doing more than speaking and something comes to be. The implication is that God envisions and sculpts each of us uniquely.

LIVING BEINGS

The text then accentuates that the LORD God "breathed into his nostrils the breath of life; and the man became a living being" (2:7). I'm so glad that the NRSV renders the last word in the sentence as "being" instead of "soul." When I was little, I was taught by someone misinformed that my soul was a little part of me that would fly off to heaven when the rest of my body was put into the ground. That is to make the word much too small.

We become living beings—all of us, composed of bodies and minds and spirits—and that is why our uniquenesses shine. It is obvious as we look around the world that every particular one is his or her own being. No two are alike. Even identical twins have each an individual personality, distinctive spirits, and singular habits of the mind. You were made an unmatched being, who is truly your own peerless self.

The word *being* gives us a better sense of one into whose nostrils God would breathe His breath or Spirit of life. We are filled to saturation with God's wind! And it causes us each to be made in God's image. Of course, God is immeasurably beyond us—so infinitely creative and ingenious and wise—so we can each bear only a wee dab of the Trinity's image. It takes every single person throughout time and space to tell us all that God wants to say about Himself.

Indubitably, thinking about this overwhelms us with gratitude and wonder. Imagine that just a minuscule flake of God is enough to fill us to saturation with individuality. Ponder what delight that gives to each of our lives. We do not have to pretend anything to try to be special. We only need be ourselves with all the God-image we channel to the world.

FORMED TO GLORIFY GOD

Immediately, as I contemplate the itsy bit of God that is mine to transmit to others, I muse about the meager but magnificent Godness in everyone. It would change the way we treated others if we kept remembering the Trinity in each one we meet.

Thus, this initial crafting of the man gives us two directions for our own formation as we read the Scriptures. It deepens our worship and adoration to consider the breathtaking (yes, and breath*giving!*) ardor of God when He shaped us. We join the psalmist in celebrating,

> For it was you who formed my inward parts;
>   you knit me together in my mother's womb.
> I praise you, for I am fearfully and wonderfully made.
> Wonderful are your works;
>   that I know very well.
> (Psalm 139:13-14)

The other guideline for our own formation is the basic honoring of other persons, suggested above. Imagine a world without racism, classism, nationalism, ageism, or any other kind of division caused by someone or some group not honoring God's breath in each of us. Assess how many wars in the history of humankind could have been prevented if no band of people ever judged another crowd as less worthy than themselves. Meditate on how it would increase your love for others to recall God's deliberate design and development of them.

Putting these two aspects of formation together more than doubles their effects, for surely, when we honor ourselves more highly because we do not disparage an exclusive sculpting of God, then we are less threatened by others and do not feel that we have to compete with them. Our particularity frees us to delight in the matchless wonder of others.

THE MAKING OF A WOMAN

In this second creation account, the animals and birds seem almost like a literary foil to enable us to realize how much the man needed human companionship. The same pattern as in Genesis 1:26 of God speaking heightens our anticipation. This time God says to Himself that it is not good for the man to be alone—or separated and by himself. Being all-wise and Three-in-One, God knows that the man needs a helper who will be a partner. We realize that this will be an expansion of the first creation account, which simply recorded that the image of God was both male and female.

In this account God now makes all sorts of animals and birds with the same deliberate formation out of the ground that led previously to the shaping of a man. The man is given the opportunity to name them all and thereby to ascertain that none of the creatures could be the kind of helper that would truly be a companion to him. Now, for the first time, there is no article *the* before *adam,* so we can read the second half of verse 20 as "but for Adam there was not found a helper as his partner."

These literary accentuations certainly refute those who think that the Bible is patriarchal. In a society and surrounded by cultures that tended to be rather male dominated, Genesis 2 is astonishingly pro-woman. Not only in the setting that has been already sketched, but also in the specific details examined below, the crafting of a woman is unusually extraordinary.

First, the man was put into a deep sleep. In the original Hebrew the word for "sleep" in verse 21 is not the customary one. This word indicates that a supernatural agency caused it to happen. As I wrote this, I laughed because into my mind flashed the blissful relief from pain that I experienced immediately when I was anesthetized after breaking my leg last summer. I wonder what sweetness the man experienced under a divine anesthetic.

Next, God took a rib from the man and, beginning with it, "fashioned" (NASB; sidenote, "Lit., *built*") a woman. The latter verb indicates again a special kind of fabrication—not just constructing a road or tunnel, but building a house or a temple, an exquisite process that must have been accompanied by some elation. Then, after tailoring the woman, the LORD God personally escorted her to the man.

The man subsequently exclaimed,

"This at last is bone of my bones
   and flesh of my flesh;
this one shall be called Woman,
   for out of Man this one was taken."
(Genesis 2:23)

This is the first time in the Bible that male and female image-of-
God bearers are actually given the names Man and Woman. Footnotes in the NRSV point out that the Hebrew word for man is *ish* and
for woman is *ishshah*. I like to joke that the fashioning of a woman
added the appreciative "ahhhhh" to humankind.

One final detail (I saved the best for last) about the making of a
woman is critically important for my point that the Bible is anything but patriarchal. The woman is called "helper corresponding"
(NASB sidenote). The adjective is rendered as "suitable" in the NASB
main text, but "corresponding" ties in better with the unexpected
name *Helper*.

I was struck a few days ago in my morning reading of Psalm 46
with the appearance of "help" (NRSV) for the LORD in verse 1. The
original Hebrew word is employed seventeen times in the First Testament to name God, or *YHWH*. Three times the name designates mili-
tary assistance. The only other uses are here in Genesis 2:18 and 20.
What an elevating honor for the woman to be named with a term usually applied to God!

That is why it is necessary to add the adjective *corresponding*. God
is a Helper superior. If one of the animals or birds had been an appropriate partner for the man, the creature would have been an infe-
rior helper. But the woman is a perfectly equitable companion, a
helper who corresponds to the man. There is no hierarchy, but she is
one who sustains and assists in a partnership of equals.

Perhaps if the first creation account was meant to show the importance of the Sabbath as its pinnacle, then the concluding creation of the woman was meant to be the high point of the second

account. You can be the judge of that.

It seems, though, that the Bible is specifically working against the patriarchalism that surrounded its time of writing. The woman is fashioned as the perfect, equal partner. Even more lovely to me, she is escorted to her first encounter with the man by God Himself.

HUMAN SEXUALITY

So far, from Genesis 1 and 2 we have learned many lessons about keeping God as the focus of our readings and about our worship in response. We also have seen models of God's actions that we want to imitate, such as the keeping of a holy rest day and providing food and water for all. The LORD has given only a few commands, and these have to do with tilling the earth and having dominion in the Trinity's way, so that all creatures are suitably fed and the earth's inhabitants are kept in harmony.

Now for the first time at the end of Genesis 2 we study an unmistakable ethical description that arises from the narrative. The word *therefore* introduces us to God's definitive design for human sexuality. The actuality that this unambiguous behest is not given as a command (as in "Thou shalt"), but simply as a matter of fact ("a man leaves . . . and cleaves . . . and they become one flesh"; v. 24 NASB) shows that this observance, communicated to us out of the perfection of creation, is the gift of a gracious God.

GOD'S PERFECT DESIGN
I think it is momentously meaningful that God's design for human sexuality is given to us before the account of the Fall, since the text doesn't speak about the thorough enactment of that design until Gen-

esis 4. The timing signifies that the description is given to us not as a means to curb the ill effects of the Fall, but as God's perfect vision of what is best for humankind. If we want as much as possible to live in the bliss of Eden, following the Trinity's intention for our sexuality will give us our best chance.

The text once again rebuts the arguments that the Bible is patriarchal. If it were, the instruction would be for the woman to leave. As it is, the man is to forsake his life centered in his family of origin in order to cling primarily and exclusively to his wife. I just happened to see an advice column today in which a woman complained that her husband's family kept pushing them to have children, though she felt not yet mature enough in their married life. This is a common problem in which the "leaving" hasn't sufficiently transpired.

The second directive of "cleaving" involves absolute loyalty and total commitment. Our society puts too much stress on romance and affection as the most vital elements necessary for a good marriage, but sometimes the ardor might wane. God's usage of the word *cleave* here indicates that one's will is more important than feelings. To cleave to someone is to stick with that person no matter what might happen.

The best example of cleaving that I've ever heard was a man caring for his wife with Alzheimer's for many, many years (if I remember right, it was twenty-five). The radio host interviewing him asked what it was like for such a long time to empty bedpans for and to touch tenderly a person who didn't respond appropriately or at all. He answered, "I can't say anything but that it was a joy." We probably all know couples like that who have been married for such a long time that their cleaving is profoundly deep, solid gold.

Because of God's design in this creation of the man and the woman, genital union now finds its rightful place, but no one should miss the obvious proper order. Full expression of one's genital sexuality—to become one flesh with another—is right only between a man and a woman and only if they have already left their families of origin and have become totally committed to each other.

A scholar familiar with Jewish tradition once informed me that the notions of leaving and cleaving indicated a specific ritual. This is suggested, too, by John the Baptist's comments about being the Bridegroom's friend (John 3:29), whose job it was to wait at the bride's house to protect her until the groom came to take his betrothed from her family to be joined with him. If such a rite is involved, that has enormous implications for our lives today.

The last verse of Genesis 2 gives us this description of the man's and the woman's innocence: "And the man and his wife were both naked, and were not ashamed" (Genesis 2:25). They were totally open to each other; free from any sort of guilt, they had no need to hide anything from each other—or from God. The nakedness and lack of shame implies a freedom to be entirely unfeigned and honest with each other. This, too, has extensive consequences—both practically and spiritually—for relationships in our times.

NORMATIVE TEXTS

The Genesis 2:24 ordering of sexual directives coming out of God's creation of a man and a woman is so important that Jesus repeats it in Matthew 19:4-6 and Mark 10:6-9 to underscore that divorce is contrary to God's best design. It is also repeated in the Pauline letters in 1 Corinthians 6:16, to warn against prostitution and fornication, and, in great contrast, in Ephesians 5:31, to hold up marriage as an image for the mystery of Christ and His Church. All other commandments about sexuality in the Bible are congruent with this first one in the second creation account.

For that reason, we can tell that Genesis 2:24 is normative for our lives. By that we mean that it is always true, universally applicable.

There are many statutes and commands in the Bible that were never meant for us or are no longer true for us. Some of these are Instructive texts—such as God's specific directions to Israel about marching around the city of Jericho (Joshua 6:2-5). Some of these mandates are Corrective texts—such as the apostle Paul's injunctions to the people in Corinth to be careful about eating food sacrificed to idols for the sake of the faith of other believers (1 Corinthians 8:4-13).

Perhaps these examples are sufficient to illustrate the difference between Corrective or Instructive texts, which are limited in application to a specific time and culture, and Normative texts, such as the Ten Commandments, which are always pertinent to everyone in any time and place.

A SEXUALLY TOXIC MILIEU

For someone to accept and follow God's design for sexual union only within a covenant, committed relationship is increasingly difficult in the twenty-first century in North America particularly and in the rest of the world. How can young persons (or older adults, for that matter) keep choosing purity, celibacy, and sexual faithfulness when they are bombarded constantly in our poisoned society by crass advertisements with immodestly dressed models, sexually explicit movies, grossly overt genital language in text messages and music, and pornographic magazines and sites on the Web?

As we have learned in this book, either positive or negative behavior fosters matching character traits. Suppose that a young girl constantly wears very revealing clothing; does she not dishonor her own body and invite others' disrespect too? Each time someone allows himself to view pornographic materials, does he not foster attributes of exploitation? Whenever an individual uses sexually explicit language, doesn't she continue to harden herself against the mystery and beauty of God's precious design for sexuality?

Meanwhile, I have found in my travels to various communities around the world that Christians (and nonbelievers too) of all ages are eager to hear an alternative to the constant sexual innuendo of the media that lambastes us. When the usual habit for many people is to go to bed with their dating partner (even on the first meeting), some of us still believe that God's way, revealed in the Bible, results in greater freedom and delight. It seems to me that our world is desperate for what the Christian community has to teach about godly sexual character.[1]

LIVING GOD'S DESIGN TODAY

When Christ is born in us by the Spirit's power, we are set free by His sexual confidence and chasteness to live according to God's design for genital union. Jesus loved His mother and His friends (and enemies!) profoundly. He had extremely close male and female friends, but He loved them with the kind of social sexuality that we discovered in chapter six.

Our trust in the Trinity's embrace frees us to love others more fully with triune kinds of love—fostering deep relationships that involve solid friendships without any sexual innuendo, family ties that are tightly knit, Christian communities that share mutual goals in God's mission.

Thus we are supported to be able to save genital involvement until we can follow our Creator's design—remaining celibate until we have left our family ties and joined our spouse in total commitment before we engage in sexual union. Throughout our youth and before our day of marriage, each time we choose to remain sexually faithful (to our known or unknown future spouse and to God) we grow in that kind of character.

Other virtues, such as patience and peace, will also contribute to a godly sexual character. We will continue to grow in faithfulness also as we continue to read the Bible, for it displays many positive and negative behaviors that will enable us to see the results of various choices. Furthermore, the Scriptures are valuable because they expose the sexual idolatries that have endured throughout human history. The narratives of both Testaments additionally demonstrate the intertwining of other kinds of idolatry—greed, power mongering, covetousness—with sexual idolatry.

As Christians we seek positive virtues and behaviors not because we ought to, should, or must, but because they are modeled for us in Jesus, whose Spirit empowers us to follow in His way. We choose to live according to the design of the Creator because the Trinity invites us to the delights of such truthfulness. Moreover, we can enthusiastically invite others to participate in those choices also because we know that thereby they will be happier, more fulfilled, more whole. This chapter is just a beginning. I pray that you will go beyond it to ponder how your various choices nurture in you a godly sexual character. Perhaps you can encourage your local Christian community to do more to foster in young people a deeper understanding of God's design for healthy and lasting expression of their genital sexuality. May we all by our chastity and sexual faithfulness offer hope to those drowning in our society's toxic sexual milieu.

HUMAN POSSIBILITY TO CHOOSE OTHER WORSHIP

God didn't want robots! If He were going to enjoy genuine fellowship with the man and the woman, it had to be by their consent and willingness. God had to provide other alternatives to worshiping only Him. No one wants to be loved solely because the other is under a requirement. Indeed, God knew prior to crafting us that there was an immense likelihood that we would choose those other possibilities for worship, that we could crave other loves. Consequently, the Trinity had to decide to forgive us and to engage together (all Three Persons) in the thorough process of atonement by which we might be reconciled through Christ before creating us in the first place.

I don't understand that, but who can fathom the magnificent creativity and sovereignty of God and hold in tension with them the Trinity's limitless wisdom and love, and the necessity of free will for human beings? To ponder this combination leads us to greater worship and adoration because of the incomprehensibility of God and His extraordinary grace.

This is a dialectical tension that leads to many other questions about our Christian faith. How can God keep giving human beings free will and at the same time love them so much that He wants everyone whom

He has created to be in relationship with Himself? How can the Trinity be sovereign over the cosmos, and yet people are free to make choices that lead to hatred and hostility, destruction and violence?

In connection with our praise for God, we need to examine the possibility made available to us to choose other worship—not to question God's wisdom in giving us the option, but to grow in humility as we wrestle with why we would wish to turn away from God. Let's be careful to read diligently exactly what God said to the man (and thereby to the woman).

GOD'S COMMAND

The biblical narrator tells us the details of the planting of the garden in Eden into which the man would be put: "Out of the ground the LORD God made to grow every tree that is pleasant to the sight and good for food, the tree of life also in the midst of the garden, and the tree of the knowledge of good and evil" (Genesis 2:9). Immediately after those details we are also told about the rivers the LORD provided for the setting.

Then, after the LORD God puts the man into the garden to till and keep it, He gives the man this command: "You may freely eat of every tree of the garden; but of the tree of the knowledge of good and evil, you shall not eat, for in the day that you eat of it you shall die" (vv. 16-17).

It is important that we read these two passages side by side to see the abundance of God's endowment. The man was not given just two trees from which to choose. He was blessed with a profusion of trees, and all of them were "pleasant to the sight and good for food" (2:9). In addition to that bounty, there were two more trees, one for life and one for knowledge. From only one plant—out of the outright plethora—was the man forbidden to eat.

THE COST OF OBEDIENCE

Why is it that we want the one choice out of multitudes that is not good for us? Why do we crave to disobey, especially when we have been warned about the consequences?

I hesitated to write and include this chapter because I have no answers to those murky questions. However, it became clear to me that we should at least ask and ponder the unanswerable queries too.

Not only were all the other trees good for food, but there was another uncommon, named tree to notice, besides the one from which the man was commanded not to eat. That was the tree of life, which was in the midst of the garden. Both special, named trees were an enigma to the man.

At this point, he didn't really know what life was all about. He didn't yet have a partner, so in his aloneness (could he have been lonely if the garden was perfect at this point and if he had a conversational relationship with God Himself?) he probably couldn't very much imagine the glorious opportunity that the tree of life presented to him. He perhaps didn't perceive, as we do now after the coming of Christ, that life in God means perfect worship and the unsurpassed rest of existence completely aligned with God's purposes through cheerful obedience to God.

Neither could the man have genuinely comprehended at this point what the knowledge of good and evil could entail. No evil existed on earth; couldn't one know about it without being engaged in it?

My questions reflect our own propensity to sin. Sometimes we think that we should learn about the sins of the world around us so that we can stay away from them. However, we can easily get caught up in them if we get too close to them. That is why the apostle Paul calls us "dear friends" and warns us to "flee from the worship of idols" (1 Corinthians 10:14). What would we have done if we had been confronted with God's command to the man to refrain from eating from the tree of the knowledge of good and evil?

A TRAGIC CHOICE

I have two simple goals in this chapter. One is to behold the immensity of God's grace and love. God gave human beings a choice more than fair. There were plenty of possibilities in the garden for pleasure and nourishment in accordance with God's design. We can't help but thank God for His mysterious and bounteous grace when we pay close attention to the setting of Genesis 2, as we have in this and previous chapters.

The other goal is that we would recognize how difficult was the position of the man (and thus the woman). Rather than blame him and her for causing so much trouble in the world, we realize that we probably—most surely?—would have made the same tragic choice. We are going to ponder the specifics of that choice in the following chapter, but here we feel daunted by the possibilities and our inadequacies. In response to that realization, we are spurred back to worship.

Oh, God, how much we need You! The choices are too grave for us to think that we can get along without You. Develop in us the necessary humility to become the people You want us to be—assiduously dependent on Your wisdom in all the alternatives of our lives. Thank you for giving us so many options for good. Set us free from any enslavements we might have to any of our preferences. Liberate us to worship You only and wholly. Amen!

THE NATURE OF SIN

It is significant that in the Bible sin is not initially defined. Instead, we are introduced to the nature of sin by a narrative, just as we similarly became acquainted with the prodigious gifts of creation in Genesis 1 and 2. Elements in all three accounts help us to perceive what we might not otherwise have observed. By means of the story in Genesis 3 we can face into the reality about humankind that is too large—and too devastating—to comprehend completely.

For example, the serpent is not explained. It is not yet understood as Satan, who doesn't appear in Hebrew literature as a separate being until after the Babylonian Captivity. In fact, the serpent is identified with Satan only in Revelation 12:9 and 20:2.

All that we are told is that the serpent was "more crafty than any other wild animal" (Genesis 3:1). As such, it acts like "the satan" or "the accuser" (Hebrew *ha-satan*) in the book of Job—somewhat like what the French call an *agent provocateur* or English speakers name a "devil's advocate," someone who asks questions to incite another's actions. Let us observe diligently the details of the narrative in Genesis 3 and record what else we can discern.

"WHA-AT'S HAPPENIN'?"
Notice in the following dialogue at which points the woman is wooed

into various attitudes by the sly serpent's questions. The cunning reptile's initial subject is, "Did God say, 'You shall not eat from any tree in the garden'?" (Genesis 3:1). The sinuous aspersion is that "God must be some sort of callous crank if he (I purposely didn't capitalize that *he*) doesn't let you have any of this beautiful fruit."

The woman seems to rush to the Lord God's defense when she answers, "We may eat of the fruit of the trees in the garden" (v. 2), but the venom has definitely grazed her. Why else would she add to God's command, "You shall not eat of the fruit of the tree that is in the middle of the garden, *nor shall you touch it,* or you shall die" (v. 3, emphasis Eve's)?

Haven't we all done that? (I know I have.) When we think we've been "unfaired against," we try to make what someone else said or did to us seem more unjust than it was. However, let's not forget what was emphasized in the previous chapter—that God had given the human beings a choice much more than fair.

Seeing that it has partially snagged the woman, the serpent now frames a fivefold suspicion to make her doubt God far more than superficially. "You will not die," it insists, which makes her distrust God's truthfulness. "For God knows," it continues, which rouses jealousy that God hadn't let her in on the secret. "When you eat of it your eyes will be opened," it asserts, and fills her with both desire and confusion, for she had thought her eyes were already open. "And you will be like God," it tantalizes, which of course sounds the most promising of all. The reptile's final snare is that to be like God means "knowing good and evil" (vv. 4b-5), which may in the Hebrew idiom mean knowing everything from A to Z or, more specifically, knowing the truth of transgression. By now the woman suspects God's goodness entirely; why has the Lord withheld all this from her? The most alluring phrase has been that to eat of the tree would make her "like God." What could be wrong with that?

Pondering the fivefold suspicions planted by the serpent, we ascertain, moreover, that all these insinuations are too coercive for us. We need help from outside ourselves to conquer our misgivings. We need some sort of assistance from beyond ourselves to sort through what we truly know. We can't rescue ourselves from our basic sinfulness or from our particular sins of mistrust and misbelief.

At this point the woman, in her naiveté, is pictured somewhat as a child with a stove. She doesn't comprehend how bad this exchange has been and what evil it leads to, but she knows the stove (or eating from the tree) will hurt. The child had trusted that her mother knew what she was saying when she warned her against touching it, but something now makes her doubt whether the hurt is greater than the value of the choice to touch. Similarly, in the woman's perfection there had been a contentment, but now this dialogue has made her feel like something is missing in her life—she has to touch the stove, as it were, to see what it's *really* like.

The serpent now shrewdly disappears (until God calls it to account) and leaves the insinuations to do their work. Meanwhile, the woman—and the man, too, we find out at the end of verse 6—contemplates the tree. It was good for food, a delight to the eyes, and desirable to make one wise (v. 6)—a triple temptation, the categories of which we'll consider more closely in the next chapter.

WHOM TO BLAME?

After the serpent has successfully sown all the seeds of skepticism, jealousy, mistrust, and disorder—all of which move the couple ever further away from God—it is no surprise that the woman and the man both eat of the fruit of the tree. Sin has been germinating for a while.

When it sprouts thoroughly, it bears a poisoned harvest, fruits of hiding and blame. The serpent had been right, but only for ill—their eyes are opened when they eat. The trouble is that they see only their own specific sin, and they don't realize that they also have put themselves into the realm of choices instead of dependence on God. Since they do grasp how vulnerable they are without God, they conceal their nakedness behind fragile garments of fig leaves (v. 7), just as we often try to disguise our culpabilities, our false worshipings, with self-justifications of various sorts.

Now they hide among the trees from the LORD God, with whom they'd been in close union (v. 8). It does not shock us that they seek to shield themselves, since they had turned away and disobeyed God's clear command. They didn't know what to expect.

When the LORD God questions them out of sheer grace and offers them an opportunity to confess, the blaming begins instead, and, as we also experience, the sins multiply. The LORD set the man up for simple repentance by asking, "Have you eaten from the tree of which I commanded you not to eat?" (v. 11) Instead of truthfully answering "Yes," the man blames the woman for giving him the fruit.

The LORD of love then gives the woman a chance to repent, but she in turn accuses the serpent of trickery instead, and God curses the serpent. This is a significant point to notice: in the LORD's stunning grace He curses only the serpent (v. 14) and the ground (vv. 17-18), but not the persons.

DESCRIPTION, NOT PRESCRIPTION

Much harm has come to women throughout the history of the world because of misreadings of Genesis 3 and especially of the LORD God's words in verses 14 through 19. The woman has been blamed (the pattern continues!) for the Fall into sin, even though the man was present with her and though he had been given the initial command to refrain from eating from the tree of knowledge. In addition, if we read the Bible for formation instead of information, we realize that the Bible is not only about the individuals named in the narratives, for it tells about us and our tendencies, attitudes, wrongdoings, and blamings.

We notice also that besides the cursing of the serpent and the soil, God further describes what will be some of the results of the sins already committed. The LORD does not assign any more blame to the woman than to the man.

After the cursing of the serpent, God simply tells what will emanate from the eternal strife between the forces of evil and descendants of the woman. One Offspring especially is described—One who would be severely injured in the conflict, but who would in the process deal the progeny of that old serpent a mortal blow (v. 15), which would lead to a final vanquishment at the end of time and the culmination of God's reign, God's recapitulation of the cosmos.

Now the LORD turns particularly to the woman and states what will be her struggles in the battles with evil. God does not say why He will increase the woman's pain in childbearing (v. 16a), though we might surmise that the pangs would not only lead her to humility and dependence, but also assist her in not taking the grace-gift of children for granted.

That she would desire her husband and he would rule over her is not God's prescription—He had made woman to be the partnering helper—but a description of another evil effect of the constant conflict (v. 16b). That the husband might become ruthless in ruling her is not the creation model; instead, if a husband is trying to follow God's design he would not choose to order his wife around or to bully or demean her. It is not God's will that she should be dominated by her partner.

Similarly, it was not God's initial intent that the soil would give Adam grief (in verse 17 God addresses Adam and not "the man"). However, it is because of him that the ground is cursed, and God's good creation has been spoiled; now thorns and thistles, toil and sweat are the results of his sin (vv. 17-19) until human beings return to the dust.

But the passage takes a more obvious turn toward grace in the last verses of Genesis 3. In verse 20 the man names his wife Eve (which resembles the Hebrew word for "living," as the NRSV footnote tells us). Also, in verse 21, for the third time the man is called Adam, without the particle *the* being added in the Hebrew to make the text say "the man."

Another sign of grace in verse 21 is that the LORD God Himself makes more lasting garments of skins for Adam and Eve and thereby hints at the future sacrifice of death that He will offer to clothe them and their descendants with righteousness.

The rest of Genesis 3 tells the singular story of God's removing the human beings from the garden of Eden so that they wouldn't have an opportunity now to eat of the tree of life and thus survive forever in their sinful state. How horrendous it would be to live perpetually without God and without any hope for change! How grateful we are to the LORD for this immensely graceful provision!

How devoted God is to human beings that He had prepared a way to rescue us from the power of the serpent at enormous cost to Himself. How astonishing His grace that we do not have to exist in this broken and troublesome world eternally. How can we ever begin to thank God sufficiently that He didn't curse us and give up on us in the first place?

THE FALL AND
ITS IMPLICATIONS FOR
GOD AND CULTURE

Actually, the title of this chapter is quite abbreviated. To name what the chapter is truly about would require something like this: "The Positive Implications of Genesis 1 and 2 for Our Relationships with God and the Culture and the Repercussions of the Fall in Genesis 3 for Those Same Relationships."

Much of our discussion in this book already has focused on our adoring relationship with God, so we need only briefly summarize these positive reverberations of God's work. Then, as we look to the negative consequences of the Fall, we will infer all the more deeply how indebted we are to God for His incredible grace that rescues us from all our temptations and transgressions and their ramifications.

Also in this chapter we will explore those continuing progressions to view how they intertwine and spiral into new convolutions. Once again, the end result should be fresh worship, for our expanding sense of triune love will usher us into gratitude and greater honesty.

OUR RELATIONSHIP WITH GOD

The first creation account in Genesis 1 revealed to us a picture of God and humankind enjoying Sabbath rest together in total harmony, because, with the fabrication of male and female in God's image, God declared everything very good. The second narrative of Genesis 2 doesn't exactly tell us much about the human beings' relationship with God, although God is very tender and personal in forming both of them, and the man is very grateful to be given the woman. Furthermore, neither one of them is ashamed to be naked before each other or in God's presence. It seems that we leave Genesis 2 with the man and the woman in superb fellowship with each other and with the LORD God.

We remember, however, Thomas Merton's idea from chapter three of this book that "to be an acorn is to have a taste for being an oak tree." The problem is that human beings in Genesis 3 were stirred up by the serpent into not settling for being *an* oak tree; they wanted to be *the* oak tree. It wasn't enough for the man and the woman to be like God; they wanted ultimately to be the commanding gods of their own lives.

The serpent offered an amazing list of possibilities: to not die, to have their eyes opened, to be like God, to know everything. As Art Simon says, this was "an awesome prospect! The irony was that they had been created in the image of God. Their reach for equality with God corrupted rather than enhanced that likeness for the human family."[1]

This is, I believe, what we mean by "original sin"—not that Adam and Eve sinned and so everyone bears the blame for that sin, but that we all don't settle for simply being in God's image. We all continue corrupting our likeness to God by coveting equality with Him. We all want to be gods in our own lives.

Another way to think about original sin is to acknowledge, as Martin Luther said, that all sin is rooted in unbelief. We don't trust that God can and will handle our lives fairly and well. We think we can do a better job if we take matters into our own hands. Always we are on the edge, tottering between resting in God's gracious purposes and relying on ourselves to plan and pursue our own prospects.

We see this especially in children, who wail and howl until they get what they want. They are the center of their own little worlds. They rule—and all the people around must pay them attention till their cries are stilled. Of course, we don't mind because infants cannot meet their own needs by themselves, but, as they grow up, we train them in order to restore them to contentment to have God's image in them and to rouse their yearning to repel the craving to be gods themselves.

THE THREE TYPES OF TEMPTATION

Once we recognize the dispositions that underlie our choices for behaviors, we have to explore the temptations that inflame our attitudes into actions. In God's original design of the cosmos, everything was in perfect harmony, and human beings were content to live in the tranquility of that complete concord with God. But the LORD meant them to be delightedly dependent, not rebelliously robotic. They had to be given a choice. Tragically, their choice to turn away from God led to eating from the forbidden tree, and that coerced them into too many choices for the rest of their lives—and ours.

Just recently I had the opportunity to preach for a congregation's worship services with the lectionary texts including Genesis 3:1-7 and Matthew 4:1-11. Studying those two passages, along with 1 John 2:16, enabled me to think more deeply about the kinds of temptations that come to us all.

Perhaps we can ruminate on the similarities of these texts if we set up a chart:

Genesis 3:6	Matthew 4:3-8	1 John 2:16
the tree was good for food	make these stones bread	the lust of the flesh
a delight to the eyes	throw yourself down from the pinnacle	the lust of the eyes
desirable to make one wise	all these kingdoms I will give you	the pride of life

Genesis 3 and Matthew 4 are quite obvious in their similarities, but 1 John 2:16 helps us immensely by introducing larger categories, which include the first couple's and Jesus' temptations and yet widen the range so that we see ourselves in them. Thereby, for example, people who do not usually lust for food might find themselves in other lusts of the flesh, lusts for any kind of physical gratification. That could encompass anything from oversleeping to hankering after one's neighbor to craving more alcohol or a "runner's high."

Neither of extra rest nor an athlete's euphoria is wrong, of course, if it does not lead a person away from doing God's will or from time necessarily spent with other relationships. But either could easily get out of hand and become a pernicious lust that degrades our likeness to God.

The second temptation, to some sort of "lust of the eyes," is effortlessly matched to the situation in Genesis, but is a little harder to understand in the case of Jesus. We are aided if we envision the various spectacles of history. We could, for example, think of the Roman hierarchy's attempts to keep the people satisfied with plenty of "bread and circuses." Or acknowledge television's ongoing need to make programs increasingly violent and more blatant in sexual exposure and expression. The tempter urges Jesus similarly to "make a scene," so that the crowds will be attracted to Him.

I thought of the lust of the eyes yesterday when I read an article featuring some of the glamorized foods involving such high prices that to order them in a restaurant assures the elite that others will notice and recognize their enormous wealth—such as those who pay forty dollars for an embellished small bottle of water. It's not the food they crave so much as it is the sensation they make. Oh, if only they would instead give that money for the sake of the poor!

The third source of sin, "the pride of life," signifies any inordinate ambitions or aspirations outside of God's will. For humans to covet God's wisdom or power, or for Jesus to seek to control all the kingdoms of the world the speedy way instead of through the suffering and sacrificial way, involves a haughtiness that elevates one's self above God. Our narcissisms always thrust us outside of relationships with the LORD and with others.

Each of these three—the lust of the flesh, the lust of the eyes, and the pride of life—is in essence narcissistic. We focus on ourselves and our desires and, as a result, move away from God. As we explored in chapter one of this book, our culture aggravates extremely our tendency to be so "curved in" on ourselves.

The reverse is also true. Our human unbelief has led to environmental and cultural destructions. Think, for example, of the many ways that human fears, demonstrated by hiding from God, aggravate community perversions. Human beings fear others with a different ethnic background and go to war against them—leading to ruination of the land and severe damage to aspects of the other people's cultural heritage.

And what about cultural artifacts in the first place? Some of them are produced purposely to attempt to be like God (like the Tower of Babel in Genesis 11). Everything in a culture is such a mix—do we imagine and invent because of the lust of the eyes or the pride of life, or is our resourcefulness directed toward God's glory? How can we discern whether cultural commodities or our uses of them lead us toward worship of ourselves or others, or the materials themselves, or God, the Creator of all that is good?

RELATIONSHIPS WITH CULTURE

The very first items of culture—that is, the products and enrichments of human endeavors—were flimsy garments of fig leaves. As time progressed, human beings (gifted by God) invented all sorts of good and bad things to combat the difficulties of thorns and thistles and labor pains. We notice in those fabrications the grace of God, who provided so many resources in our environment and gave us the model of His thorough creativity to imitate.

God's grace is obvious again, of course, in the Trinity's prevention so that human beings would not eat of the tree of life and live forever in the brokenness of our environment and culture since the Fall. It makes me wonder, however, how much of the world's culture has been developed in the misguided attempt to eat from the tree of life. What I mean is that many human accomplishments demonstrate the endeavor to build a certain kind of prominence or property that will last forever.

Throughout history, various cultural conditions have amplified temptations and multiplied sins in different ways. For example, in the time of Jesus, the Herodians sought power (the pride of life) by aligning themselves with King Herod. Meanwhile, the Pharisees thought they could rescue the Jews by teaching them to observe the Torah to perfection. The Zealots sought to overthrow the government of Rome, while the Essenes pulled away into a private community of purity. All were looking for very different forms of authority, and all could take their methods too far.

Still in our time we fall into political illusions. Today, for instance, some people speedily succumb to the notion that if we simply (or slightly underhandedly?) elect the right person, the nation's problems would be solved. They forget—how promptly!—that every leader is a sinner and will make mistakes.

My point is solely that temptations take a multitude of forms in various cultural epochs, but basically they are the same old three, with the attitudes we examined in the previous chapter preceding them. The results of sin, nonetheless, are intertwined with others from different realms of the culture and thus become inflated exorbitantly.

Each spiraling of sin has moved us and our world increasingly away from God. As a product of the Fall, initially the creation no longer perfectly fulfilled its design, and by our time, for example, the firmament no longer contains the necessary ozone levels for human safety because of human overconsumption and a host of other ecological devastations.

In many cases, "nature" seems to have turned against humankind as a result of the various ways sins have violated it. The harmony inaugurated and praised in Genesis 1 is unraveled first with the Fall of Genesis 3 between man and woman, humans and creatures, and

humans and God. Now our sinfulness has proliferated the disintegra-
tion of all relationships on a global scale.

Ponder, as an illustration, the destructions wrought when fallen
human beings with a lust to make more money do not let animals live
"according to their kind." Perhaps we have all seen news reports of
the terrible physical and affective sufferings of sows who are not per-
mitted in agribusiness to give birth among other sows and in a bed of
hay as would be their wont, because more money is made if they are
confined to reproduction crates.

We don't have space in this book for copious examples, but these
few can suffice to give us several chains of thought to pursue tracing
the developments and multiplications of the complexities and consequences of sin. Perhaps the following few questions will suggest other
avenues of analysis.

We have seen that thorns and thistles, toil and sweat were the results of sin. For everyone labor will involve some kind of struggles.
How do our attempts to relieve those strains initiate new ones?

Human beings were not allowed to eat from *every* tree. Are there
some elements of God's good creation that are not good for us and for
the LORD's purposes through us? Contemplate human inventions—
are they all good for us? Is it for our welfare and the welfare of the
world, as an illustration, if technological tools can go against the
grain of natural products? What criteria can we use for cultural
choices so that we can determine if God's creations and human inventions are good for us?

How do we avoid simply making "consumer" choices? Can good
food, lovely appearances, or the desire to be wise serve for God's glory?

Eric Sandras suggests that sin arises because of the tension between mystery and humankind's longing for the security of understanding.[2] We cannot rest in the mystery of God's wisdom for our
lives, but we want to know the particulars of how things will work
out. Do you identify with his discernment of the tension?

I know that often I don't trust God (Martin Luther's notion of unbelief) when bad things happen to me (like breaking my leg), and I

want to know exactly how the LORD will bring good out of it. I think that I would feel more secure if I could just understand all such problematic things. This tendency reflects the plight of Adam and Eve. Realizing this makes me much more sympathetic toward them and much more humbled before God.

And envisioning the various forms of narcissism sketched in this chapter makes me all the more grateful that the LORD God loves us still. How astonishing it is that, before announcing any of the negative results of the Fall (except the serpent's), the LORD proclaimed that through His own suffering the tempter would be defeated!

GOD'S DESIGN TO
OVERCOME REBELLION

When I began working on this book, I wanted to name it something like *(Almost) Everything I Needed to Know for My Christian Faith I Learned from Genesis 1–3*, to play off the famous work by Robert Fulghum about kindergarten.[1] However, to do so would focus on us rather than on God. To read the Bible properly, as we discussed in chapter one, is to begin with God and to consider how we, as a result, are being formed by the Trinity for wonder and worship, rather than emphasizing the intellectual dimension of our human faith. Besides, in order to have a thoroughly trinitarian Christian faith we would need especially the Gospel narratives to teach us the entire witness concerning Jesus and His life, teaching, miracles, suffering, death, resurrection, ascension, and the sending of the Holy Spirit.

But we have enough in Genesis 1–3 to immerse us in the general direction that God will always move, and we sample enough of His character to realize we can unceasingly trust Him. Darkness cannot overcome the power of the Light, and the works of culture (impermanent fig leaves) will be transcended by the reforms of the LORD God. The false worship of human beings is countered by new visions of the Trinity's uncustomary grace.

THE STORY OF GRACE

Throughout the first two chapters of Genesis we reveled in God's unmatchable creativity. Human beings might imagine or invent certain ideas or material objects, but God is the only One who can truly create something out of nothing. Furthermore, the Trinity is the only One who can cause everything to function in perfect harmony.

When human beings break this accord by their sinful attitudes, actions, and accusations, the LORD God is the One who takes the initiative to move the cosmos in a different direction. In Genesis 3:8-9 God is the One who comes seeking, taking a walk in the cool breezes of the evening. God has been pursuing us ever since—especially in the forms of Jesus the Christ becoming incarnate to search for the lost and of the Holy Spirit continuing the gentle brooding over us of Genesis 1:2.

In Genesis 3:11 the LORD God demonstrates enormous patience to create an opportunity for the man to confess, and He has been patient with His people and with the earth ever since. Right now, when the United States is using its money and power for destructive purposes rather than to aid the poorest people of the world, I'm quite amazed that God continues to be patient, rather than calling the nation to account. Meanwhile, however, the LORD is raising up countless people to participate in His ongoing work to reverse the attitudes and actions that bring such injustice.

Most important, the LORD God proclaims to the serpent (with the woman thereby hearing the Good News about her Offspring) that in the fullness of time its head would be struck. It would cause the Offspring suffering in the process, but it would be defeated. Such grace that God already had a plan to conquer sinfulness and sins! There is indeed hope for the rebirth or consummation of the initial creation designs, for the recapitulation of the cosmos under Christ the Head.

We get more scenes of grace at the end of the Genesis 3 narrative, as we have already seen in chapters fifteen and sixteen of this book, but the full story of God's preparation for the coming of the Offspring doesn't begin until the founding of a Chosen People through Abram in Genesis 12. Then the rest of the Scriptures tell the convoluted story of God's people obeying and disobeying, being rescued and being recommissioned, following Jesus and denying Him, failing to live in love as the Church could and being empowered by the Spirit to spread the gospel throughout the world. When read from a perspective centering on God, this is the narrative of extravagant grace, love, and mercy in their fullness surrounding human setbacks. Immersing ourselves in the flood of God's generosity propels us to praise.

BARRIERS TO READING TRUTH

It is important that we note the inundation of that grace, because so many in our world deny it or deem it insufficient. The prime obstacle to believing in God's love, numerous people say, is that sufferings—and evil in the first place—exist in the world. As was mentioned in chapter three of this book, the dialectical truth that God is both good and almighty clashes with the presence on earth of afflictions and adversities, tragedies and death.

As was also said in chapter three, if we begin with trust that God is indeed both good and almighty, then we will look elsewhere for the reasons behind suffering. We could say that because we were about to discover the goodness of God's creation, the absolute harmony of His design, the tenderness of His fabrication of the man and the woman. By beholding both the cosmic and the personal dimensions of God's handiwork, we can't help but perceive the magnificence of His power and the grandiosity of His love. Perhaps those who say there couldn't be a God if there are evil and suffering need to be pulled out of themselves enough to perceive and ponder all God's works in earth and sky and history.

If we begin from the human side of the question instead, we immediately notice that all of us are afflicted with the original sin of wanting to make ourselves gods. Though we might start by wondering how human beings could have fallen to the tempter's wiles, soon we detect the same intensifying attitudes in ourselves—fearing that God has been unfair with us, questioning His wisdom, doubting His truth, pining for more status than to be in His image. Some people facing up to these realities about themselves are moved to humility and new openness to letting God be God concerning suffering and evil.

That is especially important to observe because it seems that only in the wealthy West has suffering become a major reason to doubt God. In most poorer nations of the world, tribulation is an impetus toward faith and a clinging to the comfort of belief. Does our affluence make us presume that we can buy understanding? Has our pride caused us to place ourselves equal with God?

Finally, we return to the character of God and the subject of mystery. Many of God's purposes cannot be understood because of our inadequate comprehension of all the factors involved and because of our limited time frame, but there is no doubt in the Scriptures that the Trinity always functions out of love and mercy. In that famous verse John 3:16, the text does not say that God so loved a few people here and there. In God's most significant act for the elimination of evil and the healing of suffering, the Father sent the Son by the power of the Holy Spirit because the Trinity so loved the *world* (Greek *kosmos*). Let us bow in humility before that mystery, and let us rely on, and relish, the fervency of the LORD's love.

A HERMENEUTICS OF ADORATION

Many people these days are taught in theology schools (and through the grapevine) to read the Bible with a "hermeneutics of suspicion." That means that the method of interpretation with which they read is a prevailing doubt concerning the reliability of the Scriptures. Eugene Peterson writes strongly against such a hermeneutics as follows:

> But as we narrow our eyes in suspicion, the world is correspondingly narrowed down. And when we take these reading habits to our reading of Holy Scripture, we end up with a small sawdust heap of facts.

He cites instead Paul Ricoeur's idea of "a second naiveté," which teaches us first to discriminate between the truth and falsehood, because there are plenty of lies around. Once we have distinguished truth, however, we can

> look at the world with childlike wonder, ready to be startled into surprised delight by the profuse abundance of truth and beauty and goodness that is spilling out of the skies at every moment. Cultivate a hermeneutics of adoration—see how large, how splendid, how magnificent life is.
>
> And then practice this hermeneutic of adoration in the reading of Holy Scripture. Plan on spending the rest of your lives exploring and enjoying the world both vast and intricate that is revealed by this text.[2]

His splendid advice parallels this book's accent on focusing on God and beginning with worship. These are our best tools for dealing with suffering and tribulation.[3]

THE SCRIPTURES AS WITNESS TO GOD AND GRACE

In these pages I have purposely not said anything about historical veracity because I'm trying to move Christians beyond that battle entirely. It reveals our own arrogance that we want to be proved true—that our interpretation is "more accurate" than someone else's. Rather, I have tried to show that reading the narratives of Genesis 1–3 for worship moves us into an entirely different kind of immersion in the text.

It is the type of reading called *lectio divina*, or "spiritual reading," that is a more felicitous fit because the truths of God can only be spiritually discerned (1 Corinthians 2:12-16). When we engage with the Scriptures in a trustful way, believing that they are composed of holy words capable of forming us into relationships with God and others, then we will not hurry our reading. We will give due attention to every word—knowing that words have power to permeate our lives and *become* incarnate there.

To ingest the Scriptures is like deeply breathing in country-fresh air. Its purity suffuses our lungs, is distributed to the cells by the bloodstream, and there makes possible the energy and vigor of life. As God's Word enters our minds and hearts, the truths of the Trinity give us fresh perspective, and we live in Jesus' way by the Spirit's power to the glory of the Father.

READING FOR FORMATION

You might wonder why I stress so much the way we read the Bible. It is far too easy to apply the way we peruse or skim other literature to our daily devotions. (Many times I catch myself not paying as close attention to the text as I would like.) If we usually read for information, it is hard to break the habit, and we miss the delights and warnings of God's Word to us.

I remember vividly one Sunday when I was preaching somewhere, and I asked the congregation not to follow along in their Bibles when I proclaimed the gospel, because I was using a different translation and did not want that to be confusing. Besides, I urged them, this way they could close their eyes and put all their energy into their imaginations to experience the majesty of God's theophany in Isaiah 6.

One congregation member, however, insisted on following along in his Bible to see what the differences were. He gathered some information about various renderings, to be sure, but he missed the dramatic vision of our sinfulness, repentance, and cleansing, and the stunning beauty of God's holiness. Tragically, he lost the opportunity for perhaps dramatic transformation of his life.

When we encounter the Trinity's glorious radiance, we long for it to penetrate our lives and draw us into its aura. When we realize that God is patiently seeking us still, we experience such sweet relief as we turn and leap into His loving embrace. Abundant grace provides the most exquisitely refreshing rest we will ever know.

TRUE WORSHIP,
FAITHFUL LIVES

We began the previous chapter by realizing how much we are formed for faith by Genesis 1–3. We are not only molded for worship and for basking in the Trinity's gracious character. We are also wooed into a robust love for beauty, a grateful appreciation of goodness, and a profound passion for truth.

The narratives that we have been contemplating, however, have also given us additional gifts. It struck me recently that in Genesis 1–3 we have hints of answers for all the great existential questions. The beginning of the Scriptures offers us almost all that we need to fashion a biblical worldview. Of course, they don't offer us enough detail of the central core of the Christian faith in the teaching and suffering, death and resurrection of Jesus Christ. That offers us the hope that is essential for our biblical worldview. But many other dimensions can be found in the gracious narratives of the first three chapters of Genesis.

Having a coherent worldview enables us to process whatever happens in our lives. We know where to place events—both good and bad—in our understanding of life. The results are that we are more able to cope with difficult experiences, more grateful than proud when occasions go well, more trusting that God is still in control when the world seems totally chaotic.

THE SACRED ENCIRCLES THE SECULAR

In the beginning, when God created the heavens and the earth, He fashioned an enveloping milieu, a specific garden area surrounded by four rivers, in which to place humankind. It was an environment that God had already declared was "good." God, being boundlessly greater than that particular location, was at the same time an intimately enfolding and holy habitat for human life. We live in God, in vital union with Him.

That design of God for our well-being still persists, though marred by sin. There is indeed no established line of demarcation between the sacred and the secular—because originally God made everything to be good—but the former envelops the latter. Human beings might corrupt God's good creations, but the larger truth is the goodness of the original design. That is because evil is a negation, a perverting, an impurity; it doesn't exist on its own, but by encroaching on God's good. At the end of time, when the Trinity brings the cosmos to its fulfillment and destroys evil forever, the kingdom, or reign, of God will encompass everything. Jesus, God's own Word, will be restored as Head of the cosmos. That is the meaning of the word *recapitulation.*

With this understanding that God embraces us all in His love and grace—indeed, in Himself—we can confidently frame our answers to existential questions that haunt us all in our postmodern times. The three narratives in Genesis 1–3 enable us to comprehend clearly how we fit into the cosmos.

EXISTENTIAL QUESTIONS

1. Who am I? What is my *identity?*
Each of us is a unique creation of God. Even if less-than-desirable conditions surrounded our birth or our childhood, we as individual persons were known in the womb (as Psalm 139 tells us) and loved by the LORD. We were each made in God's image, and we find our

particular identity by the ways in which we share God's likeness with the world. That might include facets of our personality, such as a zany sense of humor, or essential talents that lead to our occupation, such as a flair for teaching. Besides these basic components, which we've had from birth, we learn from the New Testament that at times the Holy Spirit endows us with particular spiritual gifts to enable us to serve God in an exceptional way.

But we know from the first two biblical narratives that we are cherished. When the world included our forebears, it was called "very good." The whole Bible then continues to tell the story of the treasure that we are to God, that He keeps seeking us always to be in a special relationship with Himself.

2. *To whom do I belong?* To whom do I pledge my *loyalty?*
This is a tricky question for many young people today because they have had perhaps several sets of mothers and/or fathers. My husband taught in an elementary school in which the greater part of the children came from unstable or broken homes. For many such individuals in the United States, the overbearing question is whether or not they are related to, or know, anyone whom they are able to trust thoroughly.

God keeps revealing Himself to be trustworthy. He unceasingly seeks us; He perpetually is patient with us. Before human beings even sinned, He had already planned the way for them to be forgiven and to become reconciled to Himself. We can always be confident that God will never leave us; we will never be disappointed if we continually remain loyal to Him.

Later in the New Testament we will find that we can also pledge our loyalty to God's people, the community of faith. At times they might fail to deserve our dependence, yet in general they will remain a community of forgiveness and grace. However, thank God that He is God. He is eternally reliable and righteous, full of grace and mercy, never failing, though His people might.

3. *Why am I here?* What is my *purpose* in life?
We have seen throughout this book that our most festive function in

life is to praise and worship God. The more we adore the Trinity and acclaim the LORD's works, the more we will fall in love with God and the more worshipfully we will live.

Second, God's sensational grace frees us to be genuinely ourselves. Since we were created in God's image, the truer we are to ourselves the more we will live in God's likeness. That means that we can pursue whatever we most deeply love with a pure heart because it will reveal the LORD's will for us.

4. What is wrong with the world? Why is there so much *disorder?*

In the narrative of Genesis 3 we detected that there is no simple explanation for sin or for all the afflictions and troubles in our lives. Instead, we discovered that it is a combination of evil forces from outside ourselves, the influence of our peers, the corrupted attractiveness of God's creations, and our own easily manipulated attitudes and actions. Most of all, we grasped that each of us has a narcissistic bent that makes us all want to be equal with God, and therefore we spoil God's perfect designs.

We ascertained, moreover, that all these factors are too forceful for us. We need some sort of help from beyond ourselves. We can't rescue ourselves from our basic sinfulness or from our particular sins.

5. How can it be fixed? What is the *remedy* for sin and evil?

We have only a hint of an answer to these questions in the first three chapters of Genesis, for it takes the whole Bible to tell us the story of God's plan for forgiveness for sin and restoration from evil. But we learn that God will definitely provide the remedy. Only later will we discover how God uses our faithful discipleship as part of His purposes for redeeming the cosmos. At the end of Genesis 3, however, we are content to leave the remedy for sin and evil in God's masterful hands.

We also learn that we will have to bear some suffering in the meanwhile, until God totally rectifies the situation into which we have put the world. Through it all, nonetheless, we know that we can trust in God's presence and assistance, for He has revealed His character of grace and mercy.

6. *Where am I headed?* What is my *goal?*
These are existential questions for which we have only the scantiest of hints in the narratives in which we've been immersed. As we ponder the texts, we feel a yearning for Eden and the intimacy the human beings had with God. In our yearning for the Garden, we perceive this truth suggested by our being made in the image of God: wherever we go in life, we ache to be reunited with God. As many spiritual directors have written, we long for our heart's true Home, God Himself.

It is not until the New Testament that more specificity is given to that general longing for union with God. Even then, however, we do not receive many details about what that will look like. Heaven is mentioned; that the Father's house has many dwelling places is alluded to. Above all, that we will be in fellowship and union with the Father, Son, and Holy Spirit is stated clearly.

But we do not know much about eternal life in all its fullness. This is a good thing; otherwise we would be so exhilarated by it we would not be able to endure continuing in this life, and God has much for us to do meanwhile.

7. *How does everything fit together?* Is there *a master story,* a "meta-narrative," that gives me an extended history?
Whether or not a person belongs to a larger narrative is again a troublesome complication for many people in these postmodern times. With our nation's record of divorce and unsettled homes and constant mobility because of unstable jobs, many don't know their own grandparents (or they know too many of them). How can persons with a jumbled history develop self-assurance in a longer story than their own by which to get their bearings?

The first three chapters of Genesis have given us the beginnings of the kind of meta-narrative we crave. Creation provides the setting for God's larger story, which is inaugurated in perfectly harmonious goodness. As we are plunged into the tragedy of sin, we wonder how God will bring about a final restoration when out of grace He banishes human beings from the vicinity of the tree of life. Throughout the story, as it develops in the Scriptures, we discern that what we appreciated in the beginning is constantly true—that it is not that God intervenes in history, but that all history takes place in God.

If we put our wee personal histories inside the Trinity's cosmic history, we realize how everything fits together in Him, and we trust that our story is safe and secure in His hands. We don't comprehend how all the parts of our lives coalesce into a harmonious whole, but we believe that God's master narrative includes each piece and that He will bring them all into final fruition.

8. *How can I survive?* When the forces of evil assail me, how do I find the *power* to protect myself?

Many people in our competitive capitalistic age think about their lives mostly as in rivalry with others. How can I be sure I get my share, or how can I make my way over against others?—these are the questions postmodernists ask. For those who live under tyranny, the questions instead are, How do I throw off the oppressor, and how can I be free?

We remember from the early narratives in Genesis that oppression of any kind, such as that of men over women, is not God's will, but rather a result of the Fall. We dare not make any simplistic recommendations here about how to respond in God's loving way to tyranny, but we do have confidence that God is patiently beside us and working for the sake of freedom. God's plan is for harmony so He works both through us and on behalf of us in the quest for genuine reconciliation and peacemaking.

For those not under oppression, but worried about getting their share, the narratives of creation show us the plenitude of God's provisions. If we live glorifying God for the abundance of His generosity, then we don't have to worry about outstripping others. Instead, we are set free by the profligacy of grace to share our resources with those in need. We can leave the need for power to God, who uses might for good purposes.

9. What do I respect? By what *values* shall I live?

What do we honor? What is important to pass on to the next generation? What do we yearn to have abide with reference and in reverence to the true, the beautiful, and the good?

In the initial creation account, we ascertained that two very significant values in connection with God's composition of the cosmos are ecological care and justice. We also want to maintain the beauty of God's universe, the goodness of His harmony, the truth of His Sabbath hallowing.

The second creation account similarly emphasized the beauty of God's fabrication of human beings, the goodness of His unity and equality, the truth of His morality. Both accounts stir us to strive to preserve the wonder and accord of what God has done. Many of our most significant values have their origin in Eden.

10. Why should I live? What gives *meaning* to my existence?

Many people who have chased after power or prestige, popularity or possessions find that the satisfaction of those fleeting pleasures in this postmodern world is exhaustingly ephemeral. People are left wondering if anything can cause life to be worth the effort.

Our contemplation of the first narratives in Genesis has established the answer to these questions: the LORD God has given us the job of tilling the ground, of joining in His work of nurturing life. By doing so, we also give honor to God.

Life has lovely meaning when whatever we do nourishes someone or something—parenting, gardening, garbage collecting, nursing, answering the telephone, plumbing, painting. The list is endless because God's creativity is unceasing. We find our meaning because our lives matter to God. That makes meaning as eternal as He is.

Any work in life (with the exceptions of killing or harming others) can become worship of God and thereby meaningful. That meaning is lost if we turn the glory to ourselves, since our lives are also transient. But if we do what we do to the glory of God, the LORD is praised and the meaning of that lasts through infinity.

11. How can there be a future when the world is in such a mess? How do I find hope?

What enables us to cope with the economic and political mayhem of our times, the tensions of our own particular lives, our struggles to go on? In the months in which I am writing, these are perhaps the most frequently asked questions. The world economy is falling apart as the U.S. economy goes into recession. Several nations of the world are in political chaos. There is a severe food shortage, which has caused terrible rioting. The suicide rate is growing among young adults. Where does one find hope?

There is immense tenderness and grace in Genesis 3:21 when the LORD God makes garments of skin for Adam and Eve, and He Himself clothes them. The very next verse includes the LORD God again talking about "Us" (capitalized in NASB). We already know from these verses and all that preceded them that ultimately the Trinity will deal with us out of grace. This is the covenant LORD, after all, whose character of loving and generous faithfulness has been manifested at several points in the narratives.

Of course we need the entire New Testament to see how the Trinity's master story brings God's purposes to culmination. The tree of life in Genesis 2–3 reappears in Revelation 22:2 bearing twelve kinds of fruit for the "healing of the nations." The whole meta-narrative of the Bible includes the chronicle of God's chosen people, the descendants of Abraham and Sarah; the incarnation of Jesus and the account of His life and ministry, passion, and resurrection; the story of the Church and its witness to the world. We are wooed to immerse ourselves in all these descriptions by the character of the God we have encountered in Genesis 1–3, and they endow us with an unshakeable hope, hope that will never disappoint us because it reaches its consummation in the restoration of the new heavens and earth and the recapitulation of the cosmos.

12. What is my center? Who is our God?

This is not one of the usual existential questions, but it lies underneath every one of them. Ultimately the kinds of answers people find will depend on whether they know that they are embraced by God. As the great church father Saint Augustine wrote, "Oh, Lord, Thou hast made us, and our hearts are restless until we rest in Thee."

True worship is to rest in God's goodness, to cease our fretting and worry, to feast on God's beauty, and to embrace His truth. In the harmonious interweaving of all the six days' creations, as we have contemplated them in this book, God's design, ordering, and almighty power are displayed. But the most important aspect of the Trinity's character that has enfolded us is the LORD's grace.

As we have noticed, God's creations all give God glory and praise by living according to their kind. If we do that, too, we will bear the image of God in the world and give witness to the fullness of trinitarian grace.

Since we were originally fashioned in the likeness of God, all our growth in faith will enable us to speak His truth, imitate His goodness, and reflect His beauty. If we have gained in our ability to praise by this meditation on Genesis 1–3, just imagine how we will image God as we immerse ourselves increasingly in the Scriptures!

EPILOGUE

CONFESSION OF SIN AND FAITH

The idea for this book originated in a presentation given for an InterVarsity graduate and faculty conference in Atlanta during the last week of December 2002. At that time, my topic was "Creation and Culture: Genesis 1–3 as Liturgy." Miroslav Volf was the respondent to my presentation. Many of the ideas sketched at that conference were greatly expanded and refined as parts of this book.

Because the theme of that event was "Following Christ" in relation to the culture, my talk there ended with a confession of faith that also included confession for sins of the culture. Here I insert a modified version of that confession to spark your own thinking about dimensions of the phenomenon of God, systemic sin, and your personal faith in the midst of a community of faith. May the result be deepened worship.

This confession is not in the slightest intended to replace the ecumenical creeds of the Church. It is appended here only for the sake of carrying this book beyond formation into expression in words and actions.

CONFESSION OF SIN AND FAITH
We believe . . .

that our God is an extraordinary God who continually creates;
   When our culture destroys, we are worshiping other gods.

that this God devised and created an orderly, harmonious world;

When our culture disrupts ecological harmonies, we are worshiping other gods.

that this God is beyond male and female, but gives us each the privilege of imaging the Trinity—by which we can escape cultural stereotypes;
    When we accept or adjust ourselves to false cultural stereotypes, we are worshiping other gods.

that this God has made males and females for true friendship in complementarity;
    When cultural hostilities keep us from that complementarity, we are worshiping other gods.

that this God cares for all creatures and has made enough food for all to eat;
    When our cultural accumulations cause others not to eat, we are worshiping other gods.

that this God of compassion invites us to protect the whole creation, too, so that all can eat;
    When cultural entertainments prevent us from seeing and responding to need, we are worshiping other gods.

that this God offers us the gift of Sabbath rest;
    When cultural pressures preclude our taking that holy rest, we are worshiping other gods.

that this God has an ordering design for our sexuality and for one-flesh unions to be protected by covenant commitments;
    When cultural attitudes toward sexuality prevail, we are worshiping other gods.

We confess our participation in the many idolatries already listed and especially
that we human beings want to be gods for ourselves;
    When cultural presumptions make us act like gods, we do not worship the true God, the Three-in-One.

We believe and pray . . .
that God has from the beginning prepared a way for our rebellions to be overcome;
Holy Father, keep us from cultural rebellions that despise your Good News!

that the God who so beautifully orchestrated creation in the first place makes ways for creation to be restored and that the tools and ethos of, and persons in, our culture can be formed to be agents of that restoration;
Holy Jesus, fashion us to be like you to serve as agents of your divine reconciliation!

that our fabrications can be worshipful and good, but that we and they are marred by the Fall, and thus they tend to lead us away from worshiping God;
Holy Spirit, inspire us so that our imagination might be used truly to worship you!

We confess our sins and pray these things
until the day when the Creator brings to completion the divine purposes;
until sin and evil are entirely overthrown and overcome;
and until all the gifts of our multiple cultures are redeemed, restored, recapitulated
into the true worship of the Triune God.
Triune God, we worship you now and forever. Amen!

NOTES

Chapter 1: In the Beginning, God

[1]This illustration was brought to my attention by Fleming Rutledge's sermon "A Way Out of No Way," in her book *Help My Unbelief* (Grand Rapids: Eerdmans, 2000), pp. 203-9.

[2]In our present society, many people object to masculine pronouns for God because they have sometimes made Christianity patriarchal, oppressive to women. I think those objections have been given more weight since we stopped capitalizing the pronouns and thereby lost a sense of the mystery that God's transcendence could also be personal. We must remember that in the Godhead only Jesus became incarnate as a male; the Father and Spirit are beyond gender, spirit. Therefore, I have returned to capitalizing the pronouns to emphasize that they signify not God's gender, but surprising relational intimacy. The words *He, Him, His,* and *Himself* thus carry a sense of the ineffable, the secret yet revealed wonder of the Trinity's immanence, manifested most clearly in the God-Man Jesus. For further discussion of this topic, see "He, His, Him, Himself" in part one of my *Talking the Walk: Letting Christian Language Live Again* (Grand Rapids: Brazos Press, 2005).

Chapter 2: Postmodern Physics and the "Law" of Worship

[1]Best used Bernoulli's law of aerodynamics to illustrate the Law of Worship, but in keeping with my opening illustration we can think here of the law of gravity in the same way.

[2]Harold M. Best, "When Is Worship Worship?" in *On the State of Church Music: V,* lectures by William Hendricks, Harold M. Best and Robert Webber (Jefferson City, Tenn.: Louis and Mary Charlotte Ball Institute of Church Music, Carson-Newman College, 1997), p. 43. See also Harold Best's book *Unceasing Worship: Biblical Perspectives on Worship and the Arts* (Downers Grove: InterVarsity Press, 2003).

Chapter 4: Scriptural Formation

[1]Thomas Merton, *Thoughts in Solitude* (New York: Dell, 1958), p. 67, cited in Art Simon, *Rediscovering the Lord's Prayer* (Minneapolis: Augsburg, 2005), p. 44.

[2]Ibid., p. 35.

Chapter 5: The First Six Days

[1]Prayer for Psalm 148, as cited in *For All the Saints: A Prayer Book For and By the Church*, vol. 3, year 2, Advent to the Day of Pentecost, comp. and ed. Frederick J. Schumacher with Dorothy A. Zelenko (Delhi, N.Y.: American Lutheran Publicity Bureau, 1995), p. 783.

[2]Walter Wangerin Jr., *In the Beginning There Was No Sky* (Nashville: Nelson, 1986).

Chapter 6: The Creation of Human Beings

[1]See my *Sexual Character: Beyond Technique to Intimacy* (Grand Rapids: Eerdmans, 1993).

Chapter 7: Formation for Ecological Care

[1]For a scholarly perspective on this issue, see Terence E. Fretheim, *God and World in the Old Testament: A Relational Theology of Creation* (Nashville: Abingdon, 2005), p. 50.

Chapter 8: Formation for Justice

[1]For more information on Bread for the World, go to <www.bread.org> or call 1-800-82-BREAD.

Chapter 10: Keeping the Sabbath Wholly

[1]Since there is not sufficient cause in this book to investigate the Sabbath, the results of that study can be learned from my books *Keeping the Sabbath Wholly: Ceasing, Resting, Embracing, Feasting* (Grand Rapids: Eerdmans, 1989) and *The Sense of the Call: A Sabbath Way of Life for Those Who Serve God, the Church, and the World* (Grand Rapids: Eerdmans, 2006).

[2]Rick Barger, *A New and Right Spirit: Creating an Authentic Church in a Consumer Culture* (Herndon, Virginia: The Alban Institute, 2005), p. 62.

Chapter 11: The Second Creation Account

[1]David Van Biema, "God vs. Science," *Time*, November 11, 2006, p. 54.

Chapter 13: Human Sexuality

[1]For further study of this topic, see my *Sexual Character: Beyond Technique to Intimacy* (Grand Rapids: Eerdmans, 1993) and *Is It a Lost Cause? Having the Heart of God for the Church's Children* (Grand Rapids: Eerdmans, 1997).

Chapter 16: The Fall and Its Implications for God and Culture

[1]Art Simon, *Rediscovering the Lord's Prayer* (Minneapolis: Augsburg, 2005), p. 113.

[2]Eric Sandras, *Plastic Jesus: Exposing the Hollowness of Comfortable Christianity* (Colorado Springs: NavPress, 2006).

Chapter 17: God's Design to Overcome Rebellion
[1]Robert Fulghum, *All I Really Need to Know I Learned in Kindergarten* (New York: Ivy Books, 1989).
[2]Eugene H. Peterson, *Eat This Book: A Conversation in the Art of Spiritual Reading* (Grand Rapids: Eerdmans, 2006), pp. 68-69, citing Paul Ricoeur's *The Symbolism of Evil* (Boston: Beacon, 1967), p. 351.
[3]For a book for those in the midst of adversity, see my *Being Well When We're Ill: Wholeness and Hope in Spite of Infirmity* (Minneapolis: Augsburg, 2008).